International Cooking for Kids

Food is the one thing that connects people globally. We all eat, we all *have* to eat, and we all *love* to eat.

We may not all speak the same language throughout the world, but we all have food in common.

Enjoy studying world cultures and traditions through cooking.

COLUSA COUNTY FREE LIBRARY

Kids Cooking Activities.com

1

International Cooking for Kids- Multicultural Recipes to Make with your Family from Around the World

In this World Studies book, kids will learn about recipes native to each country as well as other facts about different cultures. They can try some kid friendly recipes on their own which are traditional dishes from each country.

Each International recipes page includes:

• Facts about the country

• Fun country food facts

• A phrase in the native language (if possible)

• Map of country, flag or pictures of country

• International Recipes for kids to try

Cooking international recipes is a great way to get your kids involved while learning about other cultures throughout the world. Make it a family tradition and have an international night each month. You can dress up for the occasion, create ethnic food and take a trip without leaving your house.

Each country has a dinner party menu page to use for these international nights.

Disclaimer
Please see our terms of use before using this eBook.
hhttp://www.kids-cooking-activities.com/terms-of-use.html

Copyright, www.kids-cooking-activities.com

Debbie Madson, Madson Web Publishing, LLC

Table of Contents

Kids Cooking Activities.com

Kids Cooking Activities.com

Kids Cooking Activities.com

Kids Cooking Activities.com

Kids Cooking Activities.com

Kids Cooking Activities.com

Kids Cooking Activities.com

Kids Cooking Activities.com

13

Interesting World Facts

- Most bananas are grown and shipped from Central America.

- Philippines and Indonesia are the world's leading producers of coconut.

- Africa's Ivory Coast is the largest producer of cocoa beans.

- Cocoa beans are where chocolate comes from.

- Olives are grown mostly in the Mediterranean region.

- Asia is where most of the world's rice comes from.

- Most macadamia nuts are grown on the islands of Hawaii.

- Potatoes originated in Peru. Then they traveled to Spain, Italy, Europe, Caribbean and then America.

- Yogurt originated from Turkey, Greece, and Bulgaria.

- The Romans were known for eating pasta and Italy today is famous for their homemade pasta.

- Ostrich eggs are the largest eggs in the world. One ostrich egg equals about 2 dozen (24) chicken eggs.

United States of America

Typical American cooking recipes are hard to pinpoint as many immigrant groups have influenced America. This has left a wide variety of cooking recipes. Some typical American food now a days can be linked from other countries such as Italy (pizza) or Germany (hot dogs).

Different areas of America have different influences and recipes, such as Southern Cajun cooking or Chicago deep-dish pizza.

Another factor of American cooking is what is locally grown and available such as peaches in the South, olives in California, crabs from Maryland or lobsters in Maine.

AMERICA IS ALSO KNOWN FOR SEVERAL FAMOUS THINGS

• Baseball
• Fast Food
• A variety of cultures, traditions, and beliefs

LIST THREE TYPES OF WELL-KNOWN AMERICAN FOODS.

Kids Cooking Activities.com

TYPICAL AMERICAN RECIPES

GRILLED HAMBURGERS

• 1 lb. hamburger
• 1 Tablespoon Worcestershire Sauce
• Salt and pepper

Mix hamburger and Worcestershire sauce together. Season with salt and pepper. Form into patties
and grill or bake.

BEEF CHILI

• 2 16oz. cans of pinto or kidney beans
• 28 oz. can of tomatoes
• 2 lb. ground beef, browned
• 2 cloves garlic, minced
• 2-3 Tablespoons chili powder
• 1 teaspoon pepper
• 1 teaspoon cumin

Cook hamburger and drain well. Combine all ingredients together in crock pot. Cook 6-8 hours or simmer on stove for 15 minutes. Serve with cornbread.

Kids Cooking Activities.com

POTATO SALAD

• 4 medium potatoes, diced
• 2 boiled eggs, chopped
Add potatoes and eggs to serving bowl. Mix dressing ingredients (below) together in separate bowl.

Dressing:
• 1/2 Cup mayonnaise
• ½ Cup miracle whip
• 2 Tablespoons vinegar
• 1 teaspoon salt
• 1 teaspoon sugar
• 1/4 teaspoon pepper

After combining dressing ingredients, stir into potatoes and eggs. Chill in the fridge several hours
before serving.

Kids Cooking Activities.com

GREEN SALAD WITH HOMEMADE RANCH DRESSING

Ranch dressing is a common ingredient, dip or dressing in American cooking.

- 3/4 Cup mayonnaise
- 1/4 Cup buttermilk
- 1/3 Cup minced celery with leaves
- 2 Tablespoons chopped fresh parsley
- 1 Tablespoon grated onion
- 1 clove garlic, minced
- 1/4 teaspoon dried thyme
- 1/4 teaspoon celery seed
- 1/4 teaspoon salt
- 1/8 teaspoon pepper

In a bowl, combine all the ingredients. Stir together. Or in a jar or salad shaker add ingredients together. Place lid on and shake. Cover and chill until ready to use, up to 5 days. Makes about 1 ½ cups. Prepare a green salad with lettuce and chopped vegetables as desired. Toss together and serve with Ranch dressing.

BARBECUE RIBS

- 1/2 Cup water
- 2 Tablespoons sugar
- 1 teaspoon salt
- 1/4 Cup vinegar
- 1 Tablespoon mustard
- 1/2 teaspoon pepper
- 1/2 Cup ketchup
- 2 Tablespoons Worcestershire Sauce
- 2-3 lbs. pork or beef ribs

Place ribs in a roasting pan. Add remaining ingredients together in mixing bowl. Blend together and pour sauce over ribs. Bake at 350 degrees for 2 hours. Turn ribs over several times while cooking.

PHILLY CHEESE STEAK

Some famous American cooking that originated in Philadelphia, Pennsylvania.
• Rib Eye Steak cut into thin slices
• Onions, sliced
• Mushrooms, sliced
• Sliced cheese, provolone, or processed cheese slices
• Loaf of thin French bread cut in half or hoagie rolls

In a small amount of oil sauté onions, meat, and peppers. Cut bread in half and place meat and vegetables inside. Top with cheese and eat warm.

BUFFALO WINGS

This American cooking recipe can be made as spicy as you would like and is sometimes served with blue cheese dressing.
• 3 pounds chicken wings
• 2 Cups barbecue sauce
• 1 1/2 teaspoons cayenne pepper, red
• 1/4 teaspoon salt
• 2 teaspoons black pepper
• 1 teaspoon dried minced onion, minced
• 3 Tablespoons Worcestershire Sauce

In mixing bowl stir barbecue sauce, cayenne pepper, salt, pepper, onion, and Worcestershire Sauce together. Place chicken wings into a large casserole dish. Pour sauce over wings and stir to coat. Bake in the oven at 425 degrees for 1 hour.

HOMEMADE PEANUT BUTTER
- 1 1/2 Cups salted dry roasted peanuts
- 1 Tablespoon peanut oil

Add peanuts and oil to food processor or blender. Blend about 5 minutes. Place in bowl or plastic container and cover. Chill in fridge and keep for about 2 weeks.

APPLE PIE
- Two pie crusts
- 8 medium tart apples
- 1/2 Cup sugar
- 1/4 Cup all-purpose flour
- 1 teaspoon ground cinnamon
- 1/2 teaspoon ground nutmeg
- 1/4 teaspoon salt

Peel, core, and slice apples thin. In bowl stir sugar, flour, cinnamon, nutmeg, and salt together. Add apples and toss to coat. Place in prepared pie crust and top with another crust. With a fork, poke holes in the top and press the edges of the crust together along the rim of the pan. Bake at 400 degrees for 35 minutes or until golden brown.

PUMPKIN PIE

- 3/4 Cup sugar
- 1/2 teaspoon salt
- 1 teaspoon cinnamon
- 1/2 teaspoon ginger
- 1/4 teaspoon cloves
- 2 large eggs
- 1 15 oz. can pumpkin
- 12 oz. can of evaporated milk
- unbaked 9-inch-deep dish pie shell

Mix dry ingredients (first 5) in small bowl and set aside. Beat eggs in large bowl and stir in pumpkin. Then add dry ingredients. Gradually stir in evaporated milk and pour into pie shell. Bake 425 oven for 15 minutes then reduce temperature to 350 degrees and bake 30-40 minutes until knife inserted near center comes out clean.

Kids Cooking Activities.com

Asia

Asian cooking covers a large area including the countries of Japan, Vietnam, China, Thailand, Philippines, Indonesia, India, Tibet, Malaysia, Korea, and many more countries. We are grouping them together for our World Studies but feel free to focus on one country at a time in your cooking adventures.

ASIAN COOKING: FACTS ABOUT ASIA

Asia's biggest crop is rice. It is a staple food in Asia, meaning it is something they eat often. Other common Asian ingredients are fish, squid, shrimp, and octopus. The countries of Asia are mostly close to water sources like oceans, seas, or rivers so fish are easily accessible. Some Asian spices and cooking ingredients are chili peppers, garlic, coconut, soy sauce and ginger.

DIFFERENT VARIETIES AND TASTES THROUGHOUT ASIA

• Szechuan comes from West China and includes a mix of spicy, sweet, sour, and salty flavors in Chinese recipes.
• Vietnam is known for light and healthy dishes.
• Indonesia is known for cooking with seafood and coconut milk. Two things that are readily available.
• Cantonese is known for Dim Sum.

ASIA IS ALSO KNOWN FOR SEVERAL FAMOUS THINGS BESIDES GREAT FOOD

• Sumo wrestling
• Taekwondo and Karate
• Celebration of Chinese New Year
• Origami
• Feng Shui-art of decorating; to create balance and harmony
• Tai Chi-similar to yoga

ASIAN FOOD FACTS

• Fragrant Meat in China refers to dog meat. Yes, they do eat dogs.
• Dim sum means small dishes. Usually, a variety of dim sum dishes are served with tea and friends or family who sit around together to enjoy.

LEARN A LITTLE LANGUAGE

Asia has many languages which have their own beautiful characters for writing. Gohan is the Japanese word for meal.

ASIAN RECIPES

KUNG PAO CHICKEN

• 12 oz. chicken breasts, boneless, cut into ¾ inch pieces
• 1 teaspoon cornstarch
• In bowl, stir together chicken and 1 tsp. cornstarch. Set aside.

• For sauce, combine:
• 1/4 Cup water
• 1/4 Cup soy sauce
• 4 teaspoons cornstarch
• 1 Tablespoon sugar
• 1 teaspoon vinegar
• 4-5 dashes of hot pepper
sauce
Set aside.

• 1 Cup peanuts
• 1 clove of garlic
• 3-4 green onions, sliced • 1-2 green peppers,
chopped

Lightly brown 1 Cup peanuts in oil. Set aside. Sauté 1 clove of garlic, 3-4 green onions sliced, and 1-2 green peppers chopped, in oil. Set aside. Fry chicken until brown and done. Combine vegetables, peanuts, and chicken together in pan and add sauce. Cook until everything is warm and serve with hot rice.

CHICKEN LO MEIN
- 6 oz. uncooked linguine noodles
- chicken breast halves, cubed
- 1/2 Cup soy sauce
- 1 Tablespoon brown sugar
- 1 clove garlic, minced
- 1/4 Cup chicken broth
- 1 (16-oz.) bag of frozen stir fry vegetables

Cook noodles. While noodles are cooking, cook chicken pieces in a frying pan. Add soy sauce, brown sugar, garlic, and chicken broth. Stir in frozen vegetables and cook, covered, on medium. When chicken is cooked through and vegetables are tender mix drained noodles into chicken mixture. Serve immediately.

EGG DROP SOUP
- 6 Cups chicken broth
- 2 large eggs, lightly beaten
- 1 teaspoon sesame oil

Add chicken broth to saucepan and bring to a boil. In large glass beat 2 eggs and add oil. Drizzle eggs into boiling broth. Stir gently with a fork to separate eggs and cook several minutes until eggs are done. Serve immediately.

EGG ROLLS

You can stuff these however you'd like by using different vegetables and different meat. Add a sauce for dipping and kids will love to put these together and eat them up.

- 16 oz. package wonton wrappers
- 1 lb. ground beef or ground pork
- 5 Tablespoons soy sauce
- 1 can bean sprouts
- 2 green onions, sliced
- 1 carrot shredded
- Medium head cabbage finely shredded
- 2 cloves garlic, minced
- Oil to fry egg rolls in

Cook ground beef or pork and drain well. Add in garlic, green onions, shredded carrots, and bean sprouts. Cook several minutes. Add soy sauce to mixture. Pour about 1-inch oil in a wok or skillet. Heat oil to 375 degrees. Meanwhile, lay a wonton wrapper on a cutting board or flat surface. Place 1 Tablespoon of meat filling in middle. Have a glass of water on hand to moisten sides of wrapper. Dip a finger into the water and run it along the seam of the wrapped eggroll, this will seal it, so nothing leaks out. Fry spring rolls for 3-4 minutes. Turn once or twice while cooking. Drain on paper towels and fry remaining spring rolls.

**Kids can help put these together, but younger kids should stay away from the frying as to not get splattered with hot oil.

GENERAL TSO CHICKEN

If your family doesn't like hot or spicy flavor omit the hot peppers in this Asian cooking recipe.
- 3 lbs. boneless, skinless chicken, cut into chunks
- 1/4 Cup soy sauce
- 1 egg, beaten
- 1 Cup cornstarch
- 2 Cups sliced green onions
- 8 small dried hot peppers, seeds removed

Sauce:
- 1/2 Cup cornstarch
- 1/4 Cup water
- 1 1/2 teaspoon minced fresh garlic
- 1 1/2 teaspoon minced fresh ginger
- 3/4 cup sugar
- 1/2 Cup soy sauce
- 1/4 Cup white vinegar
- 1 can or 1 1/2 cups chicken broth

Prepare sauce in a jar or large measuring cup. Stir all sauce ingredients together and store in refrigerate until needed. In bowl add chicken, soy sauce, and hot peppers. Use gloves when removing seeds from hot
peppers. This is a job for an adult!
Stir in egg. Add cornstarch and mix until chicken pieces are coated. (Don't worry if the mixture looks a little odd at this point it is supposed to.). Deep fry 7 or 8 chicken pieces at a time in 350-degree oil until chicken pieces are crispy. Drain on paper towels. Repeat until all chicken chunks are fried.
In a large frying pan or wok, add 1 tablespoon oil. Heat until very hot and sauté green onions and peppers, from chicken mixture. Stir sauce mixture into onions. Cook until it thickens. If it gets too thick, add a little water. Add chicken to sauce in wok and cook until everything is hot and bubbly. Serve over rice.

PORK CHOW MEIN

- 1 Tablespoon oil
- Boneless pork cut into strips or cubes
- 1 Cup sliced carrots
- 1/2 Cup sliced celery
- 1 Cup water
- 1/4 Cup soy sauce
- 1 Tablespoon brown sugar
- 1 teaspoon beef bouillon
- 2 Tablespoons cornstarch
- 1/4 Cup water
- 1/2 teaspoon garlic powder or 1 garlic clove minced
- 1/2 teaspoon fresh Ginger
- 4 Cups fresh bean sprouts
- 1/2 Cup sliced green onions
- Chow mein noodles

Heat oil and stir fry pork until brown. Add carrots, celery, water, soy sauce, sugar, bouillon, garlic, and ginger. Cover and simmer 4-5 minutes until vegetables are tender but still crisp. Stir in bean sprouts and green onions. Combine cornstarch and water together and blend until smooth. Stir into hot mixture. Cook until thick. Serve over chow mein noodles or cooked rice.

CHICKEN SATAY (INDONESIA)

• 1 Cup unsweetened coconut milk
• 1 1/2 teaspoon curry powder
• 1/2 teaspoon ground coriander
• 1 Tablespoon soy sauce
• 1-2 cloves garlic, finely chopped
• 2 teaspoons cornstarch
• 1 lb. chicken breasts, cut into strips
• bamboo skewers, soak in water for about 30 minutes-Skewers won't burn as much if soaked beforehand.

In Ziploc bag or medium bowl add coconut milk, curry powder, coriander, soy sauce, garlic, and cornstarch. Blend together. Add strips of chicken breasts. Marinate several hours or overnight. Thread each chicken strip onto a bamboo skewer and grill. Serve with a peanut sauce.

Peanut Sauce
• 1/2 Cup half and half
• 1/2 Cup chunky peanut butter
• 1/4 Cup coconut milk (not cream of coconut)
• 2 teaspoons sugar
• 1 to 2 teaspoons red pepper flakes crushed or
¼ teaspoon red pepper sauce

Put all ingredients into a jar, add a lid and shake. Or use a bowl and whisk ingredients together.

THAI CILANTRO PASTA WITH SHRIMP

- 3 large garlic cloves, crushed
- 2 Tablespoons minced fresh ginger
- 1 bunch fresh cilantro, stems trimmed off
- 1/4 Cup dry-roasted peanuts
- 1/2 teaspoon red pepper flakes
- 1/2 Cup peanut oil
- 8 oz. bow tie pasta
- 12 oz. cleaned shrimp, cooked
- 4 whole green onions, chopped
- 3 Tablespoons fresh lime juice

To prepare the pesto, put garlic, ginger, cilantro, peanuts, and red pepper flakes in a food processor or blender and start it running. Drizzle in oil as processor runs. Stop the processor and taste, season with salt as desired. You can prepare this ahead of time and refrigerate it until ready to use. To make meal, cook pasta in large pot according to directions on package. Just before you drain pasta, add the cooked shrimp to pot, then immediately drain pasta and shrimp mixture through colander. Put the drained pasta and shrimp back in pot and stir in pesto sauce, green onions, and lime juice. Toss gently and serve immediately. This recipe makes a small batch, you can easily double it.

SWEET AND SOUR CHICKEN

- 1 Tablespoon butter
- 4 chicken breasts or pork loin, cut into cubes
- 1 can pineapple chunks (save juice)
- 1 garlic clove
- 2-3 Tablespoons soy sauce
- I teaspoon ginger
- 1 teaspoon cornstarch

Cook chicken or pork in butter. Add garlic and sauté. Drain pineapple juice into pan. Add soy sauce, ginger and cornstarch-just enough to thicken. Let simmer for several minutes, then add pineapple chunks and serve over rice. You can also cut up carrots and green peppers and cook with the chicken for this recipe.

CREAMY THAI CHICKEN CURRY

- 2 Tablespoons canola oil
- 3 garlic cloves, minced
- 1 Cup chopped onion
- 1 Cup chopped yellow or red bell peppers combination
- 1 Tablespoons curry powder
- 4 boneless, skinless chicken breasts, cut into 1-inch pieces
- salt and pepper
- 1 Cup plain yogurt
- 1/2 Cup peanut butter, extra crunchy

In a large skillet or wok, heat oil over medium heat.
When skillet or wok is hot, add the garlic, onion, and bell peppers, stirring and cooking until vegetables just start to get tender. Add curry powder and stir, cooking just 1 more minute. Sprinkle the chicken pieces with salt and pepper, then add to the skillet or wok. Stir until chicken browns. In bowl, mix together the yogurt and peanut butter. When chicken is completely cooked, add this sauce to skillet or wok and stir, cooking until everything is heated through. Taste for seasonings and adjust. Serve over hot cooked rice.

EASY KOREAN BBQ MARINADE
BY JEAN L. (IRVINE, CA, US)
- 1/4 Cup green onion, chopped
- 1/4 Cup garlic, minced
- 1/2 Cup onion, diced
- 1 Cup sesame oil
- 2 Cup sugar
- 3 Cups soy sauce

Mix the ingredients (this will yield almost 2 quarts!). Marinade about 1/2 Cup per pound of beef or chicken. Sauté on medium high, or grill until done. Keep refrigerated unused portions.

JAPAN RECIPES

RICE BALLS
Our favorite rice balls combination
• Plain Rice balls with mini meatballs kebob on the side
• Rice balls filled with marble size cooked teriyaki meatballs inside
• Rice balls with cooked teriyaki chicken or pork cube inside
• Cook a roast chicken, cool and shred. Sprinkle chicken with soy sauce
and ginger. Add to rice balls according to directions below.

TRADITIONAL JAPANESE RICE BALL FILLINGS
• Pickled plums
• Fish
• Bonito Flakes

Directions:
With our 3 Cups rice, we made 13 medium size rice balls. Hot rice is easiest to mold so once it is done cooking work quickly forming your balls.

Cook your rice. While it is cooking get the following items ready.
• Muffin scoop
• Small bowl or cup
• Fillings
• Plastic wrap
• Salt

I've found the best method for making this is the following. Layer a sheet of plastic wrap over your small bowl. When your rice is done cooking, use your muffin scoop and fill the bowl half full. Sprinkle with salt. Push your fillings inside the middle. Wrap your plastic wrap around your ball and squeeze together. Unwrap and place on a serving plate. Continue until your rice is done. Serve. If you'd like to save some for the next day's lunch wrap the balls in plastic wrap again and store in refrigerator.

SIMPLE VEGETABLE SUSHI ROLLS

Sometimes called nori or maki rolls, these bite-size packets require little technology and kids can easily master how to make them. Small bamboo mats called makisu are required to make these rolls –the mats can be found in any Asian market or well-stocked supermarkets. Use this recipe as a good opportunity to teach kids how to cut raw vegetables and make rice.

- 1 bag carrot sticks or mini-carrots
- 1 bunch asparagus
- 1 pkg. nori sheets, roasted or cooked
- 3 Tablespoons sushi vinegar
- 3 Cups water
- 3 Cups sushi rice, cooked
- Wasabi paste (optional)

SUSHI ROLLS

Let the kids measure 2 cups of sushi rice into a bowl. Rinse the wash about three times by stirring in cold water and pouring off the cloudy water. Set in a colander to drain. Meanwhile, start preparing little piles or stations for sushi assembly. Put water in a bowl to moist your hands while spreading the sushi rice. If using wasabi, place a few spoonfuls in a nearby bowl and cover, for easy access, (remember to warn the kids how spicy it is!) Half the nori sheets and store in a zipper bag to keep moist.

VEGETABLE SLIVERS

Let older kids help with slicing if you're comfortable with them handling sharp knives. This recipe only contains asparagus and carrots, but you may want a wide variety of vegetables. Cut the carrots thinly to get translucent pieces. Cut asparagus only once to make same length as the nori sheets. Slightly steam the asparagus, for not more than 2 minutes. Add vegetables to the top of your nori sheet with rice. Roll up and slice.

Kids Cooking Activities.com

Australia

Simple, tasty, creative, and colorful, Australian food recipes are different from other dishes around the world. Many of the dishes are healthy and incorporate fruits or vegetables but you can definitely find recipes that cater to your sweet tooth. Some of the meat in Australian meals also differs from that which others are accustomed to, as bison, buffalo, and even kangaroo are among the types of meat in a number of recipes.

COMMON AUSTRALIAN INGREDIENTS

• Vegemite, spread made from yeast extract
• Meats such as kangaroo, buffalo, sheep, pork, poultry, emu, ostrich, and seafood
• grapes, bananas, oranges, and other fresh fruit grown here

Kids Cooking Activities.com

FACTS ABOUT AUSTRALIA
• 6th largest nation in the world but a small population
• 1/3 of Australia is desert
• Many unique animals can only be found here in the wild such as kangaroos, koalas, and platypus
• Home to the deadliest snakes and spiders in the world

AUSSIE FAVORITE FOODS
• Sausages
• Meat pies
• Icy poles (popsicles)
• Milo (a drink like hot chocolate)

LEARN A LITTLE LANGUAGE
• G'day - Hi
• Peckish - Hungry
• Crickey! - Surprised at something

Even if you can't get go Down Under, a few authentic Australian food recipes will have you feeling "fair dinkum."

AUSTRALIAN RECIPES

AUSTRALIAN BREAKFAST

You're probably thinking breakfast is breakfast, so how different can Australians make this meal? For starters, they have taken the American concept of pigs in a blanket to create sausage rolls, or puff pastries stuffed with pork sausage and onions. Lemon myrtle yogurt and muesli think yogurt and granola with a twist, and strawberries and cream bread are other unique breakfast items that Australians enjoy.

To make the **strawberries and cream bread,** which feeds ten, you need 15 minutes to prep the ingredients and an hour to bake it at 350 degrees. The ingredients for this recipe include:
- 1 3/4 Cups of flour
- 1/4 teaspoon of baking soda and cinnamon
- 1.2 teaspoon of baking powder and salt
- 1/4 Cup of light brown sugar
- 1/2 Cup of softened butter
- 1/2 Cup of sour cream
- 3/4 Cup of sugar
- 2 eggs
A teaspoon of vanilla
- 1 1/4 Cups of fresh strawberries, chopped or blueberries
- 3/4 Cups of walnuts, optional

In a mixing bowl, combine the flour, baking soda, cinnamon, baking powder, and salt. In a small bowl, beat the butter until it is creamy, add the sugar, and beat one minute. Add the brown sugar; beat in the eggs, sour cream, and vanilla, then stir into the flour mixture only until it is moist. Put
in the berries and nuts, pour the mix into a greased eight by four-inch loaf pan, and bake. Let it sit for ten minutes before taking it out of the pan and placing it on the rack to cool.

CHICKPEA AND TAHINI SALAD

Among the recipes for lunch are kangaroo burgers, vegemite sandwiches, and chickpea and tahini salad. It is unlikely you are going to make a kangaroo burger and a sandwich with yeast extract spread in it may not sound too appetizing, so here is the salad recipe. Not only ready in 15 minutes, but it's healthy. To make this salad, you need:

• A can of chick-peas, rinsed and drained
• A sliced red onion
• 2 chopped tomatoes
• 1 clove of garlic, crushed
• 2 Tablespoons of water
• Chopped mint, and coriander leaves
• 3 Tablespoons tahini
• Fresh squeezed lemon juice

Put the chickpeas, onion, tomatoes, mint, and coriander into a bowl. In another bowl, put the tahini, garlic, water, and lemon juice and whisk them together. Toss the chickpea mixture with the tahini mixture, dish, and serve.

FAIRY BREAD

• Sandwich bread
• Butter
• Sprinkles

This easy recipe is a favorite for kids in Australia. Spread butter over a slice of sandwich bread add sprinkles on top of butter. Cut into slices and serve.

PAVLOVA

- 4 egg whites
- 1/4 teaspoon cream tartar
- 1 Cup sugar
- 1 teaspoon vanilla extract
- 1-2 Cups berries

Beat egg whites and cream of tartar until soft peaks form. Add in sugar and continue to blend until stiff peaks form. Gently stir in vanilla extract.

On a silpat or parchment paper lined cookie sheet, add spoonfuls of dough to make individual pavlovas or add all the mixture to form one circle.

Bake in a 275-degree oven for 1 1-1/2 hour until hardens. Allow to cool in the oven. Top with fresh fruit.

Great Britain

The United Kingdom covers the countries of England, Scotland, and Wales. For this British cooking page, we will just be covering England.

FOOD FACTS ABOUT UNITED KINGDOM

• A full English breakfast includes at the very least, eggs, sausages, toast, and potatoes.
• Teatime is traditionally British and can include biscuits, scones, or little sandwiches.
• The United Kingdom is famous for their fish and chips.
• Fish and chips are a favorite when going to the United Kingdom. These are simply fried fish and French fries.

UK IS ALSO KNOWN FOR SEVERAL FAMOUS THINGS

• Big Ben
• Beautiful scenery
• Old traditional castles; some still open for tourists
• Red Double Decker buses

LEARN A LITTLE LANGUAGE

• British of course speak English but here are a few British phrases
• Blimey-expresses surprise
• Grub- means food
• Easy Peasy-Something is easy or simple to do

BRITISH RECIPES

SHEPHERD'S PIE
- 1 lb. ground beef
- 1 onion grated or finely chopped
- Vegetables sliced thinly
- Shredded cheese
- Mashed potatoes, already prepared

Sauté ground beef with chopped onions. Add vegetables desired, such as sliced carrots, peppers, or celery. Place in a casserole dish. Top with shredded cheese and spread mashed potatoes over the top. Bake at 350 degrees for 30-40 minutes until browned.

ROAST DINNER
This is often a British Sunday dinner served with roasted vegetables and a homemade gravy. The leftovers can be used for Shepherd's Pie. You can use the recipe above for Shepherd's pie. Just substitute roast meat for the ground beef.
- 1 beef roast
- Potatoes, cut in cubes
- Carrots, sliced
- 1 onion, quartered
- 1 Cup water

Add all ingredients in a crock pot or roasting pan and bake in the oven. You can add as many carrots and potatoes as desired and different vegetables such as green beans or parsnips can be added. Serve with a homemade gravy if desired.

SHORTBREAD
- 1 Cup sugar
- 1 Cup shortening
- 3 eggs
- 2 teaspoons cream of tartar
- 2 teaspoons baking soda
- 3 Cups all-purpose flour
- 1 1/2 teaspoon vanilla extract

In a mixing bowl combine shortening and eggs together. Mix in cream of tartar, flour, vanilla, and baking soda. Knead dough several minutes. Roll dough out with a rolling pin. Cut out with a rectangle or other cookie cutter. Place on a cookie sheet and bake at 350 degrees for 10-12 minutes.

TRIFLE PUDDING
This British cooking recipe is kid friendly and one that kids can put together simply.
- Sponge cake, angel food cake or other ready-made or homemade cake
- 1 can of fruit, whatever desired, save the juice
- 2 Cups custard or pudding
- Whipped cream
- Chocolate bar

Cut cake in pieces or slices. In a glass bowl, so you can see the layers of the trifle, lay cake pieces on bottom of dish. Pour the fruit, including the juice in the can, over the top of the cake allowing the juice to soak into the cake. Spread custard or pudding (either homemade or store bought) over the top of the fruit. Spread whipped cream over the custard layer. With a vegetable peeler peel pieces off the chocolate bar. Sprinkle chocolate flakes over top of whipped cream.

Kids Cooking Activities.com

CINNAMON SCONES

This British cooking recipe is great for teatime.

• 1 Cup sour cream
• 1 teaspoon baking soda
• 4 Cups flour
• 1 Cup sugar
• 2 teaspoons baking powder
• 1/4 teaspoon cream of tartar
• 1 teaspoon salt
• 1 Cup butter
• 1 egg
• 4 teaspoons cinnamon

In mixing bowl combine flour, sugar, baking powder, cream of tartar and salt together. Add in butter and blend together until mixture resembles fine crumbs. In separate bowl add sour cream, baking soda, egg, and cinnamon. Stir together then add to flour mixture. Stir just until mixture is moistened. Knead dough 5-10 times but not more than that as you don't want to handle the dough too much. Pat dough into a rectangle shape on a cookie sheet. Cut dough into wedges. Dust each wedge with a cinnamon and sugar mixture. Bake at 375 degrees for 15-20 minutes until golden. Serve with jam or butter.

Caribbean

Caribbean cooking can encompass a wide area of islands including Anguilla, Antigua, Bahamas, Barbados, Belize, Bermuda, Cayman Islands, Virgin Islands, Costa Rica, Cuba, Dominican Republic, Grenada, Guadeloupe, Haiti, Jamaica, Puerto Rico, and many more. Full of island flavor, Caribbean food recipes combine African, French, Spanish, Amerindian, and East Indian cooking styles. Goat meat and rice are staples in Caribbean food, so much so that goat water stew is the national dish of Montserrat. Saltfish, pigtails, and pigeon peas are among some of the other common Caribbean dishes.

The Caribbean's tropical climate provides common ingredients such as mango, lime, avocados, and coconut.

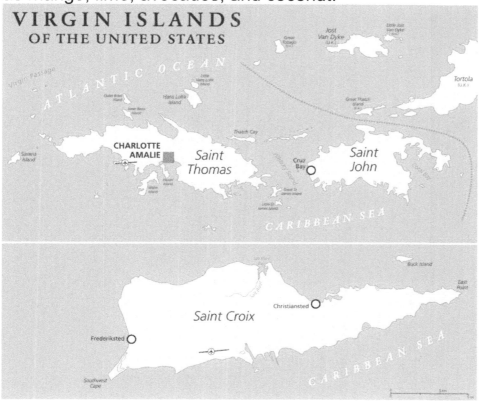

FACTS ABOUT CARIBBEAN

• Most food has to be imported
• Hurricane season is between June 1-November 30
• Caribbean relies heavily on tourism for their economy

CARIBBEAN IS ALSO KNOWN FOR SEVERAL FAMOUS THINGS

• Great for snorkeling, exploring and breathtaking views
• Exotic plants and wildlife
• White sand beaches

CARIBBEAN RECIPES

CARIBBEAN RICE
- 1 Tablespoon oil
- 3/4 Cup shredded coconut
- Heat oil in fry pan and add shredded coconut. Toast several minutes stirring often. Add:
- 1/2 Cup onions, minced
- 2 Cups rice

Stir until rice is glassy looking. Add
- 4 Cups chicken broth

Bring to a boil. Then turn to medium-low. Cover and allow to cook until tender. Before serving add in:
- 1 mango, peeled and cubed

TRINIDAD CUSTARD
- 1 can of condensed milk
- 3 eggs
- 3/4 Cup evaporated milk
- 1 teaspoon vanilla, sugar, and grated ginger

Beat eggs and add remaining ingredients. Blend together and pour into a pie plate. Bake 350 degrees for 40 minutes or until a knife comes out clean.

AVOCADO SALAD
- Black beans
- Corn
- Shredded cheese
- Sliced avocado

Dressing:
- 1/3 Cup olive oil
- Juice of 2 limes
- 1/4 Cup white wine vinegar
- 1 teaspoon yellow mustard
- 1 clove garlic, minced

Stir all dressing ingredients. Serve on the side or drizzle over top of avocado salad before serving. Serve with chopped lettuce if desired.

JERK CHICKEN
- 1 can chunk pineapple save juice
- 2 Tablespoons molasses
- 2 Tablespoons soy sauce
- 1/2 teaspoon allspice
- 2 drops of hot sauce
- Chicken breasts, cut in cubes or whole

In Ziploc bag add juice from pineapple, molasses, soy sauce, allspice, and hot sauce. Add chicken breasts. Seal Ziploc bag. Marinate in the fridge 3-5 hours. Grill or bake in oven. Serve with pineapple chunks and chopped green or yellow peppers.

CARIBBEAN SUNSET PORK CHOPS

- 1 Cup water
- 1/2 Cup lemon juice
- 1/2 Cup finely chopped onion
- 1 Tablespoon packed brown sugar
- 1 Tablespoon chopped green onion
- 1 Tablespoon canola oil
- 1 teaspoon salt
- 1 teaspoon ground allspice
- 1 teaspoon ground cinnamon
- 1 teaspoon ground black pepper
- 1/2 teaspoon dried thyme
- 1/4 teaspoon cayenne pepper
- 8 pork chops, 1/2 inch thick

Make marinade by combining all ingredients (except pork chops) in a blender or food processer and process until mixture is smooth. Remove 1/2 Cup of marinade and set aside in small bowl. Put pork chops in shallow glass dish and pour marinade over, turning pork chops to coat well. Cover with plastic wrap and put in refrigerator overnight. When ready to grill, remove pork chops and discard marinade from dish pork chops were in. Heat grill to medium heat. Arrange pork chops on grill and cook with grill lid on for 10 to 12 minutes, turning once during this time. Baste when turning with the reserved marinade.

ISLAND FRUIT AND CILANTRO SHRIMP TACOS

- 1/2 pineapple, cleaned and chopped
- 1 mango, cleaned and chopped
- 1/2 red bell pepper, cleaned and chopped
- 1/2 red onion, chopped
- 3 Tablespoons cilantro leaves, chopped
- 3 Tablespoons olive oil
- 1 Tablespoon minced ginger root
- 1 jalapeno, chopped
- 2 limes, juiced
- 1 lb. cooked medium size shrimp
- salt and black pepper

Put all ingredients in large bowl and toss gently to combine. Season with salt and pepper to taste. Serve either in taco shells or in tortilla wraps. This is equally delicious with fish, chicken, or pork instead of shrimp.

JAMAICAN VACATION JERK WINGS

- 1 orange, zest, and juice
- 1 Tablespoon grated ginger root
- 1 Tablespoon minced garlic
- 2 Tablespoons Jamaican Jerk seasoning
- 1/2 teaspoon crushed red pepper flakes
- 1/2 Cup soy sauce
- 1/2 Cup brown sugar
- 3 lbs. chicken wings
- 2 Tablespoons toasted sesame seeds

Zest the orange into a large glass bowl, then cut the orange in half and juice it into the bowl. Whisk in the ginger, garlic, jerk seasoning, red pepper flakes, and soy sauce. Add the chicken wings and toss to combine. Cover bowl with plastic food wrap and refrigerate for 1 to 2 hours, stirring a few times to make sure wings all spend time in the marinade. Preheat your oven to 350 degrees. Dump the wings along with the jerk marinade into a large baking pan. Bake at 350 degrees for 25 to 30 minutes. Remove pan from oven (leave oven on) and pour marinade juices out of pan and into a pot; return wings to oven and continue cooking for 20 to 25 minutes more or until chicken wings are thoroughly cooked.

Meanwhile, add the brown sugar to the saucepan with the liquid in it and put over low heat. Stir together and simmer slowly until mixture thickens. When chicken is cooked through, remove from oven, and pour the thickened sauce over and toss to coat. Dump wings onto platter and sprinkle sesame seeds on top and serve. (Total cooking time is about 45 to 55 minutes.)

TRINIDAD AND TOBAGO
CHEESE PASTE
BY MARTINA JACKSON
- White sharp cheddar cheese
- 1 Tablespoon mayonnaise
- 1 Tablespoon butter
- 1/2 Tablespoon yellow mustard
- 1/2 teaspoon pepper sauce

In a mixing bowl, grate the cheese with the smallest part of the grater. Add all the other ingredients and mix everything together. Cheese paste sandwiches are also a favorite at parties - awesome at kids' parties. You can be real creative with the paste when making sandwiches for kids.
Separate the paste in two to three sets, in one batch, add a drop of food coloring (red for example) and in another batch add green food coloring. Now make a sandwich using three pieces of bread and put the different colored paste on each piece of bread.

Use your imagination. When the sandwich is sliced in two or even four pieces, they look pretty. Very eye catching to kids. I used this paste as a dip (another great idea) and it can be served with your favorite crackers. Using the paste as a dip would be better served at an adult gathering.

Eastern Europe

Eastern European cooking involves some of the following countries: Belarus, Serbia, Bulgaria, Czech Republic, Hungary, Moldova, Poland, Romania, Slovakia, Slovenia, Estonia, Latvia, Lithuania, and Ukraine.

Many of these countries are covered with rows of beautiful sunflowers in the summertime, ancient architecture, world history and beautiful mountains. In the summertime you'll find fruit and vegetables are plentiful, cheap, and deliciously fresh. Eastern European cooking uses a lot of cabbage, potatoes, onions, and carrots. These ingredients are cheap and can be stored through the winter.

FACTS ABOUT EASTERN EUROPE
• Bulgaria is a leading producer of rose oil.
• Sunflower oil is highly produced thanks to the fields of sunflowers.
• Fresh fruits and vegetables are plentiful and cheap in the summertime thanks to local farmers.

LEARN A LITTLE LANGUAGE
• Dobir dehn- Good Afternoon
• La revedereh -Goodbye in Romanian
• Da-Yes

EASTERN EUROPEAN RECIPES

BORSCHT

This is a common Eastern European cooking recipe and takes a little preparation.

• Pork roast cooked and shredded or cubed
• 3 carrots, diced
• 5 potatoes, diced
• 2 beets, peeled and shredded
• Green cabbage - ½ head, shredded
• Onion, chopped
• 1-2 Cups tomato juice
• 2 chicken bouillon cubes

Wrap two beets in foil and roast at 400 degrees for 1 hour until a fork pierces the skin. Cool, peel, and shred or chop in food processor. Chop potatoes in cubes, slice carrots, chop cabbage, and chop onion. Place all vegetables in large pot. Add cooked meat and beets to pot. Cover with water and cook on medium-low for one hour. Add bouillon, tomato juice and pepper.

Taste to see if it needs anymore seasonings. Sprinkle with fresh parsley or dried parsley if fresh isn't available. **You can also add beans to the soup. Use fresh beans instead of canned. Soak beans overnight then cook them covered with water. Add a bay leaf and a quartered onion to the water. Cook 1 hour or until soft on medium heat. Drain water off and add to soup.

MOUSSAKA

A popular Eastern European cooking recipe in Bulgaria.
- 1 lb. ground beef or ground pork
- 1 onion, finely chopped
- 2 lbs. potatoes, peeled and finely chopped
- 2 tomatoes, finely chopped
- 2 Tablespoons parsley
- Salt and pepper to taste
- 3 eggs
- 1 Cup plain yogurt
- 2 Tablespoons flour

In a skillet, cook ground beef and onion together until beef is no longer pink. Drain meat and add chopped potatoes, chopped tomatoes and parsley. Salt and pepper to taste. Bake 1 hour at 350 degrees. In bowl, blend eggs, plain yogurt, and flour together. Pour over potato mixture. Bake for 10 minutes longer.

CABBAGE ROLLS

- large head of cabbage, cored
- 1 medium onion
- 2 big carrots
- 1 lb. lean ground beef, not cooked
- 1-2 Cup white rice or brown rice, cooked
- 2 bay leaves
- 2 (8 oz.) cans tomato sauce
- Tomato juice
- Sour cream, topping if desired
- Cut around the core of the cabbage.

Prepare cabbage leaves by boiling head of cabbage several minutes. Remove leaves as they fall off and continue to soften leaves until most are removed. In blender, puree carrots, 1 onion, 1/2 Cup cabbage and 1/2 Cup tomato sauce. Mix in 2 lbs. hamburger, uncooked. Add in 1-2 Cups cooked rice. Combine all together. Place meat mixture on leaf and roll up. Place in casserole dish. Add bay leaf and tomato juice or more tomato sauce. Cover with more cabbage leaves. Cook 350 degrees covered with tin foil and bake about 1 hour. Top with sour cream if desired.
Take out the core of the cabbage first and then put it in a steamer or large boiling pot of water. After about 5 minutes of steaming separate leaves. Add cabbage back to the pot of boiling water if some cabbage leaves are not easily removed. Remove thick center vein from each leaf.

Kids Cooking Activities.com

HUNGARIAN GOULASH

- 2 lbs. beef steaks, cut into cubes
- 1 onion, chopped
- 1 clove garlic, minced
- 2 Tablespoons flour
- 1 teaspoon salt
- 1 teaspoon pepper
- 1 teaspoon paprika
- 1 teaspoon thyme, dried
- 1 bay leaf
- 1 can chopped tomatoes
- 1 Cup sour cream

Toss steak and flour together in small bowl. Put steak, chopped onions and garlic into crock pot. Add seasonings including salt, pepper, paprika, thyme and bay leaf to crock pot. Add in chopped tomatoes. Stir together and cook on low 8-10 hours. Stir sour cream in soup before serving. Serve over noodles.

PIEROGI

This is typically a Polish dish, but you often find Pierogi in Russia and throughout Eastern European cooking. You can create these with whatever filling you choose. Try cooked ground beef or pork, cheese and potatoes, cabbage, or fruit fillings. They are similar to a stuffed dumpling.

• 3 Cups all-purpose flour
• 2 eggs
• 1 Cup sour cream
• 1/2 teaspoon salt

In a mixer add flour, eggs, sour cream, and salt together. Mix together to form a ball of dough. Take out of mixing bowl and knead on a floured surface 5-10 minutes. Let rest wrapped in plastic wrap for 30 minutes. Roll dough out and cut circles out of the dough by using the bottom of a glass or biscuit cutter.

Filling for Potato Cheese Pierogi

• 1/2 Cup mashed potatoes
• 1 Cup cottage cheese
• 1 onion, minced
• 1 egg yolk, beaten
• 1 teaspoon sugar
• 1/4 teaspoon salt

Sauté onion in butter. Mix mashed potatoes, cottage cheese, sautéed onion, egg yolk, sugar and season with salt and pepper.
To assemble pierogi, place a spoonful of filling on each circle of dough and moisten ends with water. Seal together by pressing with your finger or using the back of a fork. To cook, bring a large pot of water to boil. Add salt to water. Add pierogis and cook about 5 minutes. (They will float to the top of the pot). Serve this recipe with sour cream or drizzle with melted butter.

Kids Cooking Activities.com

MAMALIGA

This is a Romanian dish also seen in other Eastern European cooking. This is also known as polenta and resembles a cornmeal mush.

- 1 1/4 cups cornmeal
- 1 3/4 teaspoons salt
- 5 1/2 Cups cold water
- 1/4 Cup-1/2 cup butter, according to taste
- 1 Cup sour cream

Mix cornmeal, salt, and cold water together. Set aside. Add 4 Cups of water to a large pan and bring to a boil. Add cornmeal mixture to boiling water. Continue stirring until it thickens. Cover pan with a lid and turn heat down to low. Cook about 30 minutes. Stir occasionally. Stir in butter and sour cream. Place in a casserole dish and bake for 1 hour at 350 degrees. Top with cottage cheese or sour cream, if desired.

France

France holds an allure to many people to visit the Eiffel Tower, sit in a cafe and eat fresh hot baguettes. French food is often rich tasting and filling. Cream based sauces are in many dishes such as the Bechamel sauce recipe below. Some key French ingredients may include cream, cheeses,
wine, anchovy, tuna, tapenade (olive paste) and fresh homemade bread.

FACTS ABOUT FRANCE

• France produces a large number of cosmetics and perfume
• Families in France take a long lunch break sometimes up to 2 hours
• French cooking has an Italian influence

SOME FAMOUS THINGS ABOUT FRANCE

• Tour de France-famous bicycle race that lasts up to 3 weeks
• Notre Dame Cathedral
• Eiffel Tower
• Louvre, one of the largest art museums in the world

LEARN A LITTLE LANGUAGE

• Au revoir - good bye
• S'il vout plait - please
• Merci - thank you
• Soupe du jour - soup of the day

FRENCH RECIPES
FRENCH BAGUETTES
• 2 Cups warm water
• 2 Tablespoons vegetable oil
• 3 teaspoons salt
• 2 Tablespoons sugar
• 2 Tablespoons yeast
dissolved in I Cup warm water
• 7-7 ½ Cups flour
• Cornmeal, optional
• Egg, beaten

In a large measuring cup or small bowl dissolve yeast in 1 Cup warm water and sprinkle in 2 Tablespoons sugar. Set aside. In large mixing bowl add 1 Cup water, vegetable oil, salt and 2 Cups flour. Blend together. Add yeast mixture and remaining 5 Cups flour adding one cup at a time. Dough should form into a ball if it is too sticky add 1/4-1/2 Cup more flour. Place dough on a floured surface and knead. Divide dough in two portions if easier to handle. Knead dough 5-10 minutes until soft and smooth.
Pour 1 Tablespoon of oil in a large bowl. Add dough and turn the dough over so both sides are oiled. Place plastic wrap or a towel over the top and let rise for 1 hour. Grease a large cookie sheet and sprinkle with cornmeal, if desired. Divide dough in half and roll each half out with a rolling pin in the shape of a rectangle. (If you'd like smaller loaves divide dough in portions desired)
Roll dough up, long ways, tightly. Seal edges and with a knife cut diagonal slits on the top. Place on cookie sheet and let rise again 1 hour. Beat one egg and brush the top of the loaves with the beaten egg. Bake at 350 degrees for 15 minutes.

FRENCH CHEESE SOUFFLÉ RECIPE

This cheese soufflé recipe seems to be a little difficult but once you break it down into steps and taste it, you'll see it isn't that hard to make and well worth the effort. If you have small ramekin dishes these work great for little individual sizes for each family member. Otherwise prepare one in a large round dish for the whole family.
- 1/4 Cup butter
- 1/4 Cup all-purpose flour
- 1/2 teaspoon salt
- 1/4 teaspoon mustard
- Dash of cayenne pepper
- 1 Cup milk
- 1 Cup shredded cheddar cheese
- 3 eggs, separated
- 1/4 teaspoon cream of tartar

Grease a round casserole dish.

In a saucepan melt butter. Whisk in flour, salt, mustard, and cayenne pepper. Stir constantly on medium-low heat until well blended. Whisk in 1 Cup milk until mixture is smooth and no longer has lumps. Bring to a boil and continue stirring. Add shredded cheese and cook until melted. Set aside. In two separate bowls, add egg whites in one bowl and egg yolks in another. Beat egg whites and cream of tartar until stiff peaks form. In separate bowl, beat 3 egg yolks for several minutes. Stir egg yolks into cheese mixture. Add a small amount, about 1/4, of the egg whites to the cheese mixture. Stir together. Pour cheese mixture slowly into remaining egg whites. Pour into greased dish. Bake in a 350-degree oven for 45-55 minutes. Insert a knife in the center of the soufflé and it should come out clean. Serve immediately.

CROISSANTS

- 5 Cups flour
- 1 1/2 Cups butter, cold
- 1 Cup water warm (105° to 115°)
- 1 package yeast active dry or 1 tablespoon yeast
- 3/4 Cup half and half
- 1/3 Cup sugar
- 2 eggs
- 1 1/2 teaspoons salt
- 1/4 Cup butter or margarine, melted
- 1 Tablespoon water

Cut cold butter into smaller chunks or slices. In a mixing bowl blend 4 Cups of flour with 1 Cup cold butter. Mixture will be crumbly. Set aside. In a separate bowl dissolve yeast in warm water. Add a sprinkle of sugar to the yeast mixture. When yeast is bubbly and foaming pour into empty mixing bowl. Add 1 Cup flour, half, and half, 1/3 Cup sugar, 1 egg, salt and melted butter. Blend together then add yeast mixture and crumbly butter mixture. Blend together until just moistened. Chill for several hours in the fridge.
Take dough out of fridge after chilling and knead on a floured surface. Divide dough into 4 smaller balls. Keep the dough you aren't working with in the fridge to chill. Roll one ball into a large circle. Cut into triangles or wedge shapes. Roll the triangle up starting at the wide end and rolling up toward the pointed end. Bend ends to look like a croissant shape. Place on an ungreased cookie sheet and finish rolling remaining dough. Cover with plastic wrap or a light towel and let rise 1-2 hours.

In a small glass beat together one egg and 1 Tablespoon water. Before baking brush each croissant with egg mixture. Bake at 325 degrees for 25-30 minutes or until golden brown.

**To add fillings to croissants, place a tablespoon of filling on a triangle and roll up. Fillings could be a fruit filling, chocolate, or a cream filling.

**You can eat croissants as is or make them into a sandwich. Chicken salad or ham and cheese is great on croissants.

CREPES

Crepe is French for "pancake." They are different from traditional thick pancakes as they are thinner, often times have a filling inside and can be rolled up.

- 1 1/2 Cups all-purpose flour
- 1 Tablespoon sugar
- 1/2 teaspoon baking powder
- 1/2 teaspoon salt
- 2 Cups milk
- 1/2 teaspoon vanilla extract
- 2 eggs
- Butter or stick

margarine or shortening for cooking

In mixing bowl lightly beat eggs. Add vanilla, milk, salt, sugar, and flour. Blend together. Stir in baking powder. Let rest for 10 minutes. Heat small fry pan to very hot. Melt butter and spread around to coat pan. Add batter, just enough to cover the bottom of the pan. When the crepe bubbles turn to brown other side. Set aside on a plate. Heat pan again for several seconds then pour batter into pan. Stir batter before each crepe.

CHOCOLATE MOUSSE

- 8 ounces semisweet baking chocolate
- 1/4 Cup water
- 2 Tablespoons butter
- 3 egg yolks
- 3 Tablespoons sugar
- 1/4 Cup water
- 1 1/4 Cups whipping cream

Chop chocolate with a knife or place in Ziploc bag and use a rolling pin or kitchen mallet to crush. Whip whipping cream in a mixer for several minutes until stiff. Chill in the fridge. Meanwhile, melt chocolate pieces, water, and butter in saucepan. Stir until melted and smooth. Let cool. In clean saucepan add egg yolks, sugar and another ¼ Cup water.

Whisk together and cook over medium heat. Use a candy thermometer and continue stirring until temperature reaches 160 degrees. Turn off stove and set pan aside. Whisk chocolate mixture into egg yolk mixture. Allow to cool, stirring often. Stir in whipped whipping cream. Spoon into serving dishes and chill until serving.

BECHAMEL SAUCE
- 5 Tablespoons butter
- 1 onion chopped
- 1 Tablespoon black pepper
- 1/2 teaspoon ground cloves
- 2 bay leaves
- 3 garlic cloves, minced
- 4 1/2 Tablespoons flour
- 4 1/2 Cups milk
- 1/4 Cup heavy cream
- 1 teaspoon thyme
- 1 teaspoon salt

In saucepan melt butter. Add onion, pepper, cloves, bay leaves and garlic. Sauté several minutes. Whisk flour into butter mixture. Slowly whisk in milk and stir any lumps out. Bring to a boil then lower heat to low. Simmer for 5-8 minutes. Strain sauce through a strainer with small holes. You want to take all the onion, cloves and bay leaves out of the sauce at this point. Use on pasta, cooked vegetables, lasagna, or another easy French recipe.
**You can simplify this recipe by melting the butter and whisking in flour. Slowly add milk and stir until it thickens. Season with thyme and salt. (This isn't the typical French recipe however.)
Turn this Bechamel sauce into a Mornay sauce by adding cheese. Stir shredded cheese in your sauce.
Stir until melted. You can use this for homemade macaroni and cheese or on top of homemade pasta.

Kids Cooking Activities.com

RATATOUILLE
- 1 medium unpeeled eggplant, cubed
- 2 small zucchini, sliced
- 1 Cup green bell peppers, chopped
- 1/2 Cup medium onion, finely chopped
- 2 medium tomatoes, quartered
- 1/4 Cup olive or vegetable oil
- 1 1/2 teaspoons salt
- 1/4 teaspoon pepper
- 2 cloves garlic, finely chopped

In skillet pour 1/4 Cup oil in bottom. Heat oil and add chopped eggplant, zucchini, peppers, onion, and tomatoes. Sprinkle with salt and pepper and stir in garlic. Simmer on medium and cook for 15 minutes or until vegetables are tender.

FRENCH ONION SOUP
- 1/4 Cup Butter
- 1 clove garlic, minced
- 4 Cups thinly sliced white onions
- 6 Cups water
- 8 beef bouillon cubes
- 1/8 teaspoon black pepper
- 1/4 teaspoon Salt
- 1 bay leaf
- 1 Tablespoon Worcestershire Sauce

In a large saucepan melt butter and sauté garlic and sliced onions for 5-8 minutes until onions are tender and golden. Add water, bouillon cubes, pepper, salt, bay leaf and Worcestershire Sauce to saucepan. Bring to a boil and simmer on low for 25 minutes. Serve with toasted cheese bread or croutons. Serve warm.

CRÈME BRUELLE
- 1-quart heavy cream
- 8 egg yolks
- 4 eggs
- 2 teaspoons vanilla
- 1/2 teaspoon salt
- 1/2 Cup sugar
- 1/2 Cup brown sugar

In a saucepan heat heavy cream. Bring just to a boil and take off heat. Set aside. In mixing bowl beat 4 eggs, 8 egg yolks and 1/2 Cup brown sugar.

Add a small amount of the hot cream mixture into the mixing bowl and stir together. Then add all of the mixture in the mixing bowl to the remaining hot cream mixture in the saucepan. Stir together and add 1/2 teaspoon salt and 2 teaspoons vanilla. Stir together and pour into ramekins, small pie plates or one shallow baking dish. Fill a casserole dish with water and place ramekins or pie plates into the water. The ramekins will be covered with water up to about 1/2 way. (This is called a water bath) Bake at

350 degrees for about 30 minutes or until set. Cool. Sprinkle tops with brown sugar and caramelize in the oven before serving. You can also serve with fresh fruit.

Germany

Officially called the Federal Republic of Germany, Germany is the largest, most populated country in central, industrialized Europe, home to more than 80 million Deutschen. It is also one of the most influential members of the European Union, consistently offering a strong, stable economy supported by a socialist democracy.

Besides containing 16 distinctly different states each presenting its own exclusive culture, Germany is bordered by many countries, including Poland, Denmark, Czech Republic, Austria, France, Switzerland, Belgium, the Netherlands, and Belgium.

FACTS ABOUT GERMANY
• You can find over 1500 different types of sausages
• Levi Strauss was born in Germany-the inventor of Levi jeans
• Both composers, Beethoven and Johannes Brahms were German

GERMAN IS ALSO KNOWN FOR SEVERAL FAMOUS THINGS
• Beautiful scenery and mountains
• Germany's biggest festival-Oktoberfest

LEARN A LITTLE LANGUAGE
• Please- Bitte
• Danke - Thank you
• Good bye- Auf Wiedersehen

COMMON GERMAN INGREDIENTS

Incorporating traditional Bavarian, French and Italian food styles, German food recipes contain an interesting variety of cheeses, game meats, spices, noodles, and potato dishes. Germany is also famous for producing a wide range of breads, with the most popular bread being rye-wheat (roggenmischbrot) and whole-grain (vollkornbrot).

Das brot is an important part of German diet and thought to be necessary for good health. In addition, Germany has over 15,000 bakeries offering doughnuts, pastries, pies and, of course, breads, with many Germans visiting their local bakery for their morning breakfast. While the common belief that Germans love to eat meaty, carbohydrate-filled meals is partly true, they are also one of the fittest nations in the world due to their love of outdoor physical activity and healthy eating. People in Germany do not "stock up" on food like Americans do. Instead, they visit the neighborhood food marts where fresh vegetables and meats are always available and purchase what they plan on eating that day.

Germans favor pot roasts, sausage, and poultry over any other foods, with the average German consuming 70 pounds of meat each year. In fact, you will find around 1500 different kinds of sausages gracing German dinner tables. German food incorporates vegetables consisting of spinach, beans, peas, turnips, and cabbage. Spargel, or white asparagus, is a popular side dish as well. Sometimes spargel is served in restaurants as a meal by itself. Spätzle, or noodles containing mostly egg yolk, originates from the southwestern region of Germany.

GERMAN RECIPES

GERMAN PANCAKE

- 3/4 Cup sugar
- 4 eggs
- 2 Cups milk
- 2 Cups all-purpose flour
- 1 teaspoon cinnamon
- 1 teaspoon vanilla

In mixing bowl blend all ingredients together.
Let sit about 5 minutes. Heat a frying pan. Add
- 1 Tablespoon butter.
Pour 1/4 Cup of batter in pan and when browns flip over. Serve with powdered sugar or jam.

GERMAN SPÄTZLE

This dish is frequently served with Schnitzel and are like little dumplings.
- 2 Cups of wheat flour
- 4 to 5 large eggs
- 1 teaspoon of salt
- 1-2 Cups water
- Hot water for tossing the Spätzle
- Chopped herbs or greens, such as kale or baby spinach, optional

Mix the flour, eggs and salt in a large bowl and add the water. Blend in greens if using. After rolling out the dough, scrape thin strips of the dough into boiling water. When the Spätzle noodles rise to the surface, remove them, and put them into the hot water to avoid sticking together. After draining, place on a heated plate and serve immediately.

PORK SCHNITZEL
- 4 flat boneless pork or veal steaks
- 1 egg, beaten
- 1 1/2 Cups plain breadcrumbs
- 1/2 teaspoon paprika
- 1 Cup flour, however much you will need
- Sprinkle of pepper

In one flat dish add flour. In a separate dish add beaten egg. And in final dish add breadcrumbs, pepper and paprika. Dredge pork in flour, then beaten egg, and then bread crumbs. Heat frying pan with oil. Fry each steak.

MUSHROOM GRAVY SAUCE
- 3 or 4 medium sized sliced mushrooms
- 4 Tablespoons oil
- 1/2 bunch of chopped parsley
- 1 1/2 Cups meat broth
- 1/2 Cup cream
- One onion, finely chopped

Fry onions and mushrooms for two to three minutes. Next, add broth and bring to a boil. Add cream but don't boil. Add in the parsley last. Pour over your pork schnitzel.

Greece

Some common ingredients in Greek Cooking could be cheeses, oils, fruits, nuts, eggplant, zucchini, fresh herbs such as basil or oregano. Fish, seafood, and lamb are commonly used in Greek Cooking.

FOOD FACTS ABOUT GREECE

• The tall white chef hat originated in Greece
• Greece is known for growing olive and lemon trees
• Sheep and goats thrive on the rocky and mountainous country, which is why dishes often use lamb instead of other meat

GREECE IS ALSO KNOWN FOR SEVERAL FAMOUS THINGS BESIDES GREAT FOOD:

• Greece is made up of 2,000 major islands of Greece
• Many beautiful beaches
• First Olympics was held here over 2,000 years ago

LEARN A LITTLE LANGUAGE

• Little snacks or appetizers are called mezethes.
• Pronounced Kali Orexi in Greek means Bon Appetit.

Kids Cooking Activities.com

GREEK RECIPES

GREEK SALAD

- Feta cheese
- Chopped fresh tomatoes
- Chopped cucumbers
- Black olives
- 1 Tablespoon olive oil
- 2 Tablespoons vinegar
- Black pepper

Arrange tomatoes, cucumbers, olives, and feta cheese in bowl. Toss together gently and pour olive oil and vinegar over top. Season with pepper.

GREEK GYRO

- 1 lb. pork, lamb, or beef loin, cut in strips
- 4 Tablespoons olive oil
- 4 Tablespoons lemon juice
- 1 Tablespoon mustard
- 2 cloves garlic
- 1 teaspoon dried oregano

Mix together in bowl and marinate meat strips several hours. Grill or bake and serve in pita bread topped with yogurt sauce below.

CUCUMBER WITH YOGURT SAUCE

- 1 Cup plain yogurt
- 1 cucumber chopped
- 1/2 teaspoon crushed garlic
- 1/2 teaspoon dill weed

Marinate in refrigerator. Serve with gyros recipe above or as a vegetable dip.

Kids Cooking Activities.com

GREEK SOUVLAKI

Pork is used for this recipe, but you can substitute beef or chicken if desired.

- 1/4 Cup lemon juice
- 1/4 Cup olive oil
- 1/4 Cup soy sauce
- 1 teaspoon dried oregano
- 3 cloves garlic, minced
- 2 lbs. pork tenderloins, cut into cubes
- 2 onions, cut in chunks
- 2 green or red bell peppers, cut in chunks
- wooden skewers - soak before using to prevent burning

In Ziploc bag add lemon juice, olive oil, soy sauce, oregano, and minced garlic. Add pork cubes, onion chunks and pepper chunks. Seal and marinate in the fridge several hours or overnight. Place meat and vegetables on skewers and grill.

GREEK SPANAKOPITAS (SPINACH PUFFS)

- 1 medium onion, finely chopped or grated
- 2 Tablespoons olive oil
- 10 oz. package frozen spinach, thawed and drained
- 1/2 lb. feta cheese
- 6 oz. cottage cheese
- 3 eggs, beaten
- 1/4 Cup breadcrumbs
- 1/2 lb. phyllo pastry sheets
- 1/2 Cup butter, melted

In large pan sauté onion in olive oil. Squeeze excess water out of spinach. Add to onions. Cook over low heat several minutes. Crumble feta cheese in medium bowl. Add in cottage cheese and eggs. Stir breadcrumbs and spinach mixture into cheese. Stir together until well combined. Cut phyllo sheets into squares of 4-5 inches. Cover sheets that you are not using to prevent them from drying.

With pastry brush, brush melted butter over each square, layer several squares together and add a spoonful of spinach filling to middle. Fold top over in a triangle shape. Brush tops with butter and place on a cookie sheet. Continue with remaining phyllo sheets and spinach filling. Bake at 425 degrees for 20 minutes.

GREEK BAKLAVA

- phyllo pastry sheets
- 1 Cup butter, melted
- 3/4 Cup sugar
- 1 teaspoon cinnamon
- 2 Cups chopped walnuts
- 1/2 Cup water
- 1/4 Cup lemon juice
- 1/4 Cup honey
- 1/2 teaspoon vanilla extract

Grease an 8x11 pan and layer several sheets of phyllo in bottom, brushing each sheet with melted butter. Cover sheets that you are not using to prevent them from drying. In bowl mix ¼ cup sugar, walnuts, and cinnamon together. Sprinkle mixture over top of phyllo sheets in pan. Add remaining sheets of phyllo, brushing each sheet with melted butter. Cut squares through layers of sheets and then diagonally through each square. Bake at 300 degrees for 1 hour or until golden brown. Before baklava is done cooking, make the sauce. In saucepan add water, lemon juice, honey, and vanilla. Bring to a boil and continue stirring until sugar is dissolved. Pour over hot baklava.

India

Indian cooking relies heavily on the spices available to them in their country. Curry, rice, yogurt, and lamb are frequent ingredients in cooking. Many Indians are vegetarians eating mostly wheat, rice, and lentils. Chapati and Roti are types of Indian unleavened bread (meaning it doesn't rise).

FOOD FACTS ABOUT INDIA
- Many Indians eat from a metal plate or banana leaf
- Indians eat with their hands
- Rice is usually the main course of a meal

INDIA IS ALSO KNOWN FOR SEVERAL FAMOUS THINGS:

• Chess was invented in India
• Bengal Tiger is found throughout India and is the national animal of India
• Algebra, trigonometry, and calculus also originated in India.
• India is one of the oldest countries in the world

LEARN A LITTLE LANGUAGE

Indians greet each other by placing the palms of their hands together, bowing and saying "Namaste" in greeting.

Kids Cooking Activities.com

INDIAN RECIPES

CHICKEN CURRY

- 1 lb. chicken, cut in cubes
- 1 Tablespoon vegetable oil
- large onion, chopped
- 2 cloves garlic, minced
- 1 Tablespoon gingerroot, minced or 1 teaspoon ground ginger
- 1 teaspoon curry powder
- 1 teaspoon cinnamon
- 1 teaspoon ground cloves
- 1 teaspoons chili powder
- 1 teaspoon cumin
- 1/2 Cup fat-free plain yogurt

Cut chicken into cubes and set aside. Sauté onion and garlic in oil. Add chicken and brown. Stir in yogurt and spices. Turn to low and simmer for 20 minutes. Serve with rice if desired.

TANDOORI CHICKEN

- 1/2 Cup plain yogurt
- 1/2teaspoon salt
- 1/4 teaspoon cardamom
- 1/8 teaspoon cumin
- 1 Tablespoon lemon juice
- 1/2 teaspoon paprika
- 1/8 teaspoon ginger
- 1 garlic clove
- 1 lb. chicken legs and thighs or chicken breasts

Mix ingredients together and pour over chicken in a Ziploc bag or medium bowl. Marinate 4-24 hours. Bake, broil, or grill.

LASSI YOGURT DRINK
- 5 Cups yogurt
- 5 cardamom pods
- 6 Tablespoons sugar
- 1 Tablespoon water
- 1/8 teaspoon nutmeg

Remove seeds from cardamom pods and crush. In blender add yogurt, cardamom seeds, water, and sugar. Blend together several minutes. Before serving sprinkle each glass with nutmeg.

INDIAN KOFTA
- 1 lb. lean ground beef or lamb
- 1 small onion, grated
- 3 garlic cloves, minced
- 2 teaspoons cumin
- 2 teaspoons paprika
- 1 teaspoon ground cinnamon
- 1 teaspoon oregano
- 1 teaspoon cayenne pepper
- 1 teaspoon salt
- 1 teaspoon black pepper

Add ingredients together in a large bowl. Blend together well, by kneading with your hands several minutes. Shape into sausages and grill or bake.

INDIAN CHUTNEY
- 1/2 Cup tamarind paste
- 1/2 Cup chopped pitted dates
- 2 cups water
- 1/2 teaspoon chili powder
- 1/2 teaspoon cumin
- 1/2 teaspoon ginger
- 1 teaspoon salt
- 3/4 Cup brown sugar

Blend all ingredients together to make a thin sauce. Warm up in saucepan. Serve with kabobs or other meat.

DAL

This is often the main protein dish in Indian cooking for families who don't eat meat.

- 1 Cup lentils
- 2 Cups water + 1 Cup water
- Onion sliced
- 3/4 teaspoon garlic
- 3/4 teaspoon fresh minced ginger
- 1/2 teaspoon turmeric
- 1 Cup water
- 3/4 teaspoon salt
- 2 jalapenos peppers seeded and chopped
- 1 tomato, diced
- 2 Tablespoons cilantro
- Cooked rice

In a saucepan simmer lentils, water, and onion. Simmer over low heat for 20 minutes covered with a lid. Puree lentil mixture in blender and add in 1 cup water and salt. Put back on the stove and thicken slightly. Stir in peppers, tomato, and cilantro. Serve with rice if desired.

Indonesia

In Indonesia, some common fruit are mangoes, banana, coconut, jackfruit, and papaya. Chili peppers, garlic and fish sauce are used often in cooking as well as mint, cilantro, and basil spices.

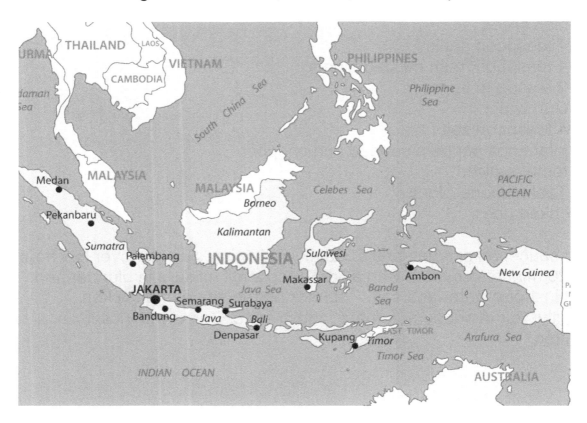

FACTS ABOUT INDONESIA

• Indonesia consists of multiple islands
• Crocodiles are farmed in this area and their skin is used for making leather bags, shoes and their meat sold within the area
• Rice, coconuts, tea, rubber, and silk are Indonesia's major agriculture

INDONESIA IS ALSO KNOWN FOR SEVERAL FAMOUS THINGS:

• Coconuts are grown here and are exported as well.
• Tropical rain forests and jungles
• Some animals that live in this area are rhinoceros, tigers, elephants, monkeys, Komodo dragons and a variety of snakes.

LEARN A LITTLE LANGUAGE

• food - makanan
• Excuse me - Permisi [per-mi-see]

INDONESIAN RECIPES
GADO GADO
- Rice cooked and set aside.
- 3 potatoes, chopped
- 3 hardboiled eggs
- 2 carrots, chopped
- 2 cucumbers, chopped
- green onions, chopped
- 3 Cups bean sprouts
- 1/2 or less Chinese cabbage, shredded

Chop and prep vegetables. Hard boil eggs and boil chopped potatoes and carrots. Mix, in a large serving bowl cucumbers, onions, bean sprouts, carrots, chopped eggs, cabbage and potatoes. Set aside and prepare sauce.

PEANUT GADO GADO SAUCE
- 1/2 onion, chopped
- 1 garlic clove, minced
- Juice of lemon
- 3/4 Cup water
- Bay leaf
- 1/2 Cup peanut butter

In fry pan sauté onion and garlic in oil. Add lemon juice, water, and bay leaf. Simmer several minutes and remove bay leaf. Add peanut butter. Stir to combine. Simmer several minutes. Drizzle dressing over vegetables or serve on the side. Serve with rice. Gado Gado could be served with a simple Teriyaki chicken on the side or mixed together.

TERIYAKI CHICKEN
- 4-5 chicken breasts, cubed
- 1/2 Cup teriyaki sauce

Marinate for several hours and cook. Serve with Gado Gado.

Kids Cooking Activities.com

Ireland

FACTS ABOUT IRELAND

• On kids' birthdays, kids get turned upside down and bump their head on the floor depending on how old they are (similar to other countries giving "birthday spanks")

• The country of Ireland consists of two areas. Ireland and Northern Ireland. Northern Ireland is part of the United Kingdom.

IRELAND IS ALSO KNOWN FOR SEVERAL FAMOUS THINGS:

• St. Patrick's Day
• Castles
• Shamrocks, green hills, lush landscapes

LEARN A LITTLE LANGUAGE

In Ireland they speak English and Irish/Gaelic

Kids Cooking Activities.com

IRISH RECIPES

IRISH SODA BREAD

Some common ingredients in Irish soda bread, besides the basic ingredients, are buttermilk, caraway seeds and baking soda.

• 2 Cups white flour
• 1 Cup whole wheat flour
• 2 teaspoons baking soda
• 1/2 teaspoon salt
• 1/2 Cup white sugar
• 2 eggs
• 1 1/2 Cups buttermilk
• 3/4 Cup raisins
• 1 Tablespoon caraway seeds

In mixing bowl combine flours, baking soda, salt, and sugar. In separate bowl combine eggs and buttermilk. Pour into dry ingredients and blend slightly, you just want the dough moistened so don't beat too long. Stir in raisins and caraway seeds with a spoon. On a floured surface knead dough several minutes. Place in a round cake pan. With a knife slice an X on the top of the loaf. Bake at 350 degrees for 30-40 minutes until golden.

IRISH COLCANNON

• 2-3 lbs. potatoes, peeled, cubed, boiled
• Cabbage or kale, shredded
• 1 Cup butter
• 1 1/4 Cups milk
• 4 green onions, chopped
• Bacon cooked and chopped

Peel, cube, and boil potatoes. Meanwhile boil or steam cabbage in water. Drain and place in a mixing bowl. Add butter and milk. Blend together. Add in cooked shredded cabbage, green onions and chopped bacon. Stir together. Add a dab of butter to each serving.

Kids Cooking Activities.com

CORNED BEEF BRISKET

- 1 onion
- Carrots cut in chunks as many as desired
- Potatoes cut in chunks as many as desired
- 1 Cup beef broth
- 1 teaspoon Worcestershire sauce
- 1 whole clove of garlic
- Bay leaf
- Cabbage cut in wedges

Place cut vegetables on bottom of crock pot. Place corned beef brisket on the top. In mixing bowl combine broth and Worcestershire Sauce. Pour over top of brisket. Add garlic clove and bay leaf. Cook on low 6-8 hours. Add cabbage to top of pot half way through cooking time.

IRISH STEW

A traditional Irish stew was prepared with the cheapest ingredients that were easily accessible. Lamb, potatoes, and onions could be found easily so they were often included in the stew. Nowadays you can find chicken, beef and any kind of vegetables included.

- 2-4 lbs. cubed lamb, chicken, or beef
- 2 teaspoons salt
- ¼ teaspoon pepper
- 2 quarts water or beef broth
- 2 bay leaves
- 1 Tablespoon Worcestershire Sauce
- carrots, peeled and cut in slices, as many as desired
- potatoes, peeled and cubed, as many as desired
- onions, sliced, as many as desired

Add ingredients to crockpot or large soup pan making sure liquid covers all meat and vegetables. If cooking in crockpot cook on low 6-8 hours or high 4-6 hours. On the stove top for one hour or oven 2 hours covered.

Italy

Italians have some of the most famous recipes that people around the world try to duplicate. Whether it is a complex recipe or a simple lasagna, Italian recipes are sure to please. Common ingredients for Italian recipes are Prosciutto, fresh mozzarella, fresh tomatoes, basil, pesto, roasted pepper, or fresh pasta. As a matter of fact, pasta was invented in Italy, as was pizza.

FACTS ABOUT ITALY

• Mealtime is family time for Italians. They gather together as a family. Local stores close for several hours and many children go home from school for lunch.

• Italy is a rather small country about the size of Arizona, USA.

• Italy is shaped like a boot.

ITALY IS ALSO KNOWN FOR:

• Art; ever heard of Michelangelo's Sistine chapel in Rome. He painted the roof of the chapel for four years, while lying on his back!
• Leaning tower of Pisa
• Bocce ball originated in Italy
• Famous cities such as Rome, Florence, Milan

LEARN A LITTLE LANGUAGE

• Buon Giorno! (bwon zhor-no) - Hello or Good Day
• ArrivederLa (ah-ree-vuh-dehr-lah) - Goodbye
• Ho fame (oh fah-meh) - I'm hungry.

ITALIAN RECIPES
EASY ITALIAN WEDDING SOUP

- 4 Cups chicken broth
- 1 Cup water
- 1 Cup medium shell pasta
- Homemade or frozen meatballs, cooked
- 2 Cups spinach leaves, finely chopped
- 2 Cups pizza sauce

In saucepan add broth and water. Bring to a boil. Then add pasta and meatballs. When pasta is tender. Stir in chopped spinach and pizza sauce. Heat through and serve immediately.

Italian wedding soup usually isn't served at weddings. It gets its name because of the fact that the spinach and the meat go (marries) well together. Sprinkle with salt and pepper.

TOMATO BRUSCHETTA

Italian bruschetta and Italian crostini are similar, but bruschetta is grilled, or toasted bread rubbed with garlic and oil. Olive oil is the key ingredient in bruschetta. Crostini also uses slices of thin bread, but they are usually served with cheese or tapenade (olive paste).

• 1 loaf Italian bread cut diagonally in slices
• 1 garlic clove; minced
• 2 Tablespoon olive oil
• 2 large tomatoes; peeled, seeded, and chopped
• 1/4 teaspoon salt
• 1/4 teaspoon pepper
• 1/2 Cup chopped fresh basil

On a cookie sheet place sliced bread. Broil several minutes until golden brown. Meanwhile stir garlic and olive oil together. Brush each bread slice with garlic oil. Spread chopped tomatoes on top of each slice of bread and sprinkle with salt and pepper. Warm in the oven. Sprinkle with chopped fresh basil and serve.

ITALIAN BREAD SALAD

- 1 loaf Italian bread
- 3 fresh diced tomatoes, save juice also
- 1 red onion, diced
- 1 3/4 Cups fresh basil leaves, chopped
- 1/2 Cup or less olive oil
- Salt and pepper to taste

Cut bread in slices and cube. You need about 4 Cups for this recipe. Place cubes on a cookie sheet and toast until golden brown stirring several times. In serving bowl, combine bread cubes, diced tomatoes, diced onion, juice from tomatoes, fresh basil leaves, and 1/2 Cup olive oil together. Toss to coat. Season with salt and pepper and serve immediately.

101

VEGETABLE LASAGNA

- Lasagna noodles, uncooked
- 1 small bunch of broccoli flowerets, cut in small pieces
- 2 carrots, shredded
- 4 Cups spaghetti sauce or large jar
- 2 green or red bell peppers, chopped
- 1-2 Tablespoons olive oil
- 15 oz or 2 Cups cottage or ricotta cheese
- 1/2 Cup grated Parmesan cheese
- 2 Tablespoons dried parsley
- 2 large eggs
- 1 Cup mozzarella cheese, for the top

Sauté garlic in olive oil and add carrots, broccoli, bell peppers and spaghetti sauce. Let simmer about 8-10 minutes until vegetables are tender. In separate bowl mix cottage cheese, Parmesan, parsley, Mozzarella cheese (save some for sprinkling on the top) and eggs. Spread a thin layer of sauce on bottom of an 8x11 or 13x9 pan. Lay lasagna noodles on bottom of pan. Spread cottage cheese mixture over top of noodles. Spread more sauce on top of noodles. Continue layering in pan until the pan is full. Sprinkle Mozzarella cheese on top and bake at 350 degrees for 35-40 minutes or until noodles are tender.

Kids Cooking Activities.com

HOMEMADE PASTA DOUGH

- 2 3/4 Cups all-purpose flour
- 1 teaspoon salt
- 3 eggs
- 1 Tablespoon olive oil
- 3 Tablespoon water

In a mixer add flour and salt. Add one egg at a time and continue beating after each addition. Add 1 Tablespoon olive oil. Continue mixing. Add 3 Tablespoons of water and mix until a ball forms. Place dough ball on a floured surface and knead dough about 5 minutes until very soft. Wrap in plastic wrap and let sit for 20 minutes. When ready, roll dough out on a floured surface. Shape dough into desired shapes or sizes. For example, cut small triangles, strips or squares for soups or cut small rectangles and squeeze together in the middle for bowtie shapes. Cook pasta in salted
boiling water until tender.

RISOTTO WITH PARMAGINAO CHEESE

- 2 Tablespoons butter
- 2 Tablespoons olive oil
- 1 medium onion, grated
- 1 lb. about 2 1/2 Cups short grain white rice
- 6 Cups chicken broth
- 2 Tablespoons butter
- 3 oz. Parmagiano Reggiano cheese, coarsely grated

In large saucepan add butter and olive oil. Allow to heat and melt butter. Add grated onion and sauté several minutes until onion is transparent. Add in rice and stir until all rice is evenly coated and glassy looking. Add chicken broth and turn stove to medium-low. Let simmer covered for about 10 minutes. Stirring occasionally. When rise is tender stir in butter and cheese. Serve immediately.

EGGPLANT PARMIGIANA

- 2 eggplants, sliced
- 2 eggs
- 1-1/2 Cup bread crumbs
- 1/8 teaspoon pepper
- 1 garlic clove, minced
- 3/4 Cup olive oil
- Large can of tomatoes
- 1/3 Cup tomato paste
- 2 Tablespoon minced basil
- 1 teaspoon salt
- 1/8 teaspoon pepper
- 1 Cup grated Parmesan cheese
- 1/2 lb. Mozzarella cheese; thinly sliced

In a flat baking dish or pie plate place 2 beaten eggs. In another dish add bread crumbs and pepper. Dip eggplant slices in egg then in bread crumbs. Lay the slices on a casserole dish or cookie sheet and chill for 20 minutes. Meanwhile in a skillet, sauté garlic in 2 Tablespoons oil. Take garlic out of pan with a slotted spoon (leaving the oil). Add tomatoes, tomato paste, basil, salt, and pepper. Cover and simmer 20-30 minutes.

In a large skillet add remaining oil. Fry eggplant slices in oil until browned on each side. Drain on paper towel. In a baking dish cover a layer of tomato sauce on the bottom. Top with a layer of eggplant slices, Parmesan, and mozzarella cheese. Continue layering in the pan. Top with mozzarella cheese and bake at 350 degrees for 30 minutes.

ZEPPOLI

- 1 package active dry yeast or 1 tablespoon yeast
- 1 Cup warm water
- 1 1/2 Cups flour
- 1-quart vegetable oil (for frying)
- 2 Tablespoons powdered sugar (for rolling in after cooked)

In a large measuring cup or small bowl dissolve yeast in 1/2 Cup warm water. While yeast is foaming and getting bubbly, pour 1/2 Cup water and 1 1/2 Cups flour in a mixing bowl. Pour in yeast mixture and mix until forms a soft dough. Knead on a floured surface several minutes. Pour about 1 Tablespoon or less oil into a large bowl. Place dough in the bowl flipping over to oil both sides of dough. Cover with a towel or plastic wrap and let rise about 1 hour. Pour 1 quart or several inches of oil in saucepan. Using a candy thermometer heat oil to 375 degrees. Form dough into small balls and fry in the heated oil. (This is a step for an adult or older chef) Take out when golden brown and drain on paper towels. Roll in powdered sugar and serve warm.

Kids Cooking Activities.com

POTATO GNOCCHI

- 1 Cup mashed potatoes
- 2 eggs
- 1 teaspoon salt
- 1 Cup cottage or ricotta cheese
- 8 teaspoons butter
- 1 Cup Parmesan or Romano cheese
- 3 Cups flour
- Freshly grated Parmesan cheese
- Pasta sauce or tomato sauce

Blend potatoes, eggs, salt, cottage cheese, butter, and Parmesan cheese together in mixer. Add in flour. Knead dough until smooth. Roll in thick ropes. Cut each rope into 3/4 inch-1-inch pieces. Place on cookie sheet sprinkled with flour. Pour water into a large pot and add salt. Bring to a boil. Place gnocchi pieces into boiling water. When gnocchi rise to the top take them out with a slotted spoon. Sprinkle with Parmesan cheese and serve with pasta sauce. Serve immediately.

ITALIAN TOMATO SAUCE

- 1 Cup onions, chopped
- 1 clove garlic, crushed
- 3 1/2 Cups tomatoes, whole, peeled
- 2/3 Cup tomato paste
- 1/2 Cup water
- 1/2 Cup mushrooms, pureed in blender
- 1 teaspoon oregano
- 1/2 teaspoon basil
- 1 teaspoon salt
- 1/8 teaspoon black pepper

In blender puree garlic, tomatoes, and mushrooms. Pour into a crockpot. Add tomato paste, water, oregano, basil, salt, and pepper. Stir together until well combined. Cook on low, 8-10 hours or overnight.

ITALIAN BISCOTTI

- 3 1/2 Cups flour
- 1 Cup almonds chopped
- 1/4 teaspoon baking soda
- 3/4 teaspoon salt
- 3 large eggs
- 1 1/2 Cups sugar
- 1/2 Cup butter, melted
- dash of lemon or orange zest
- 2 teaspoons vanilla extract
- 1 teaspoon almond extract

Combine dry ingredients in a bowl including flour, baking soda, salt, and nuts. Set aside. In mixing bowl beat together eggs, sugar, butter, zest, vanilla, and almond extract. Slowly stir in flour mixture. Blend together. Place dough on a floured surface and divide in two. Shape dough into a long loaf. Lay both loaves on a greased cookie sheet. Bake in a 350-degree oven for 25 minutes or until firm and lightly golden brown. Cut loaves diagonally into slices. Place on cookie sheet and bake another 10-15 minutes turning over once. Biscotti will become crisp and you can cool on wire rack.

ITALIAN FRITTATA

Frittata is an Italian word for omelet.
- 8 eggs
- 1/2 teaspoon salt
- 1/4 teaspoon pepper
- 1/2 Cup grated Parmesan cheese or Romano cheese
- 1/2 teaspoon dried basil
- 1/2 tsp dried sage
- 1/4 Cup diced fully cooked ham or prosciutto
- 1 small zucchini, sliced or cubed
- 2 medium green onions, sliced
- 2 Roma (plum) tomatoes, sliced
- 1 teaspoon olive oil

In large skillet or pie plate add 1 teaspoon olive oil. Spread around to coat bottom and edges. In mixing bowl beat together eggs, salt, pepper, cheese, basil, and sage. Stir in chopped ham, zucchini, and onions. Pour egg mixture into skillet and bake at 375 degrees for 15-20 minutes until the frittata is set. Top with sliced tomatoes and more Parmesan cheese.

SIMPLE ITALIAN STARTER
- 3 plum tomatoes sliced crosswise
- 2 Tablespoons fresh basil
and 2 Tablespoons fresh parsley, chopped
- Olive oil
- Salt and pepper to taste

Place sliced tomatoes on a serving platter. Sprinkle with chopped herbs and drizzle olive oil over the top. Sprinkle with salt and pepper.

BASIL AND PINE NUT ORZO

- 1 package (8 oz) Orzo
- 1 Tablespoon extra-virgin olive oil
- 3 Tablespoons pine nuts
- 1 Tablespoon dried basil
- Salt and pepper to taste

In a large pot, cook orzo until just tender, about 2 to 3 minutes, and drain. As orzo is cooking, put oil in large heavy skillet and heat to medium; add pine nuts and stir until lightly toasted, about 4 or 5 minutes. Stir in the basil, then add orzo and toss. Taste and season with salt and pepper if desired. Serve warm.

ITALIAN COOKING LESSON TIP

An easy way to make cannelloni (they resemble stuffed tubes) is to use cooked lasagna noodles.
Place the filling on top of the lasagna noodle and roll up the noodle.
Place in a casserole dish and top with tomato sauce.

ITALIAN PINE NUT PESTO WITH LINGUINE

- 2 garlic cloves
- 2 Cups fresh basil
- 3 Tablespoons pine nuts
- 1/2 teaspoon salt
- 1/2 Cup olive oil
- 1 Tablespoon chopped Italian parsley
- 1 lb. linguine
- 4 Tablespoons grated
Pecorino Romano cheese

Put the garlic, basil, pine nuts, and salt in food processor and start running, then drizzle in all the olive oil as the machine is running. Let this process until smooth for about 3 minutes. Set the pesto aside. Cook the linguine in large pot according to directions on package. Drain, reserving the water. Return the pasta to the pot and add the pesto and toss. Add a tablespoon or so of reserved water to pasta if it seems dry, then toss in the cheese. Serve hot.

ITALIAN RED SAUCE

- 2 Tablespoons olive oil
- 2 anchovy filets, finely chopped
- 4 garlic cloves, minced
- 1/2 Cup sliced ripe olives
- 2 Tablespoons capers
- 1/2 teaspoon red pepper flakes
- 1/4 teaspoon dried oregano
- 1/4 teaspoon salt
- 1 can (28 oz.) crushed tomatoes
- 1 lb. linguine
- 1/4 Cup chopped fresh Italian parsley (for garnish)

In large heavy skillet, heat olive oil over medium-low heat. Add anchovies, garlic, olives, capers, red pepper flakes, oregano, and salt. Cook, stirring constantly, over medium-low heat for 2 to 3 minutes or until you can just smell the garlic getting fragrant. Be careful not to let the garlic burn. Stir in tomatoes; lightly cover the skillet and cook 15 to 20 minutes or until sauce thickens. Serve over cooked hot linguine and top with sprinkles of parsley.

BASIL AND PINE NUT ORZO

- 1 pkg (8 oz) Orzo
- 1 Tbsp extra virgin olive oil
- 3 Tbsp pine nuts
- 1 Tbsp dried basil
- salt and pepper to taste

In a large pot, cook orzo until just tender, about 2 to 3 minutes, and drain. As orzo is cooking, put oil in large heavy skillet and heat to medium; add pine nuts and stir until lightly toasted, about 4 or 5 minutes. Stir in the basil, then add orzo and toss. Taste and season with salt and pepper if desired. Serve warm.

Latin America

Latin American food recipes encompass some of the tastiest and most colorful dishes throughout the globe. Brazilians add flavor to rice, Cubans spice up pork, and Argentineans enjoy the sweet, light flavor of their authentic lemon cookies. While each country has its own unique dishes, you can combine different elements to create true Latin American cuisine.

COMMON LATIN AMERICAN INGREDIENTS

• tortillas
• maize
• tamales
• pupusas
• salsa
• guacamole
• Pico de galla
• corn
• lima beans
• potatoes and sweet potatoes
• chili peppers
• avocados
• chocolate
• alpaca
• quinoa
• tropical fruit
• yuca

FACTS ABOUT LATIN AMERICAN

• This is the area Christopher Columbus discovered.
• This region is rich in Incas' and Aztecs' history
• Simon Bolivar is a hero of several Latin America countries as he helped countries win freedom from the Spanish.
• South America is famous for several geographic locations such as the world's highest waterfall called Angel Falls in Venezuela. It is

home to the largest river, Amazon River, the longest mountain range, the Andes, the largest rainforest, the Amazon Rainforest

LEARN A LITTLE LANGUAGE
This large region speaks Spanish and Portuguese, and some areas French.

LATIN AMERICAN RECIPES

TAMALES
• Corn husks; soak in water several hours if dry
• Mixture of pork and chicken cut in cubes and season with
  • 1/2 teaspoon cumin
  • 1/2 teaspoon chili powder
  • 1/2 teaspoon salt
  • 1/4 teaspoon pepper
  • green onions, chopped
  • 1-2 garlic minced
Combine all ingredients except corn husks. Marinate overnight.

Prep the following:
Cooked Rice
Cooked garbanzo beans
Cooked cubed potatoes
Cooked cubed carrots
Diced onions
Diced peppers
Lay out husks and layer cooked rice, cooked garbanzo beans, marinated meat, cooked cubed potatoes, cooked cubed carrots, diced onions, diced peppers, and more rice. Make sauce below and drip sauce over top.

Sauce:
To make sauce stir 1-2 Tablespoons of your sauce from the marinade with white corn flour-Spanish type mix. Roll up husks and tie with twine. Pour more sauce in the top of your husk. Put tamale in saucepot. You want your tamales to steam so put rocks on the bottom to lift them from the bottom. Lay tamales perpendicular in order to not block the steam. Steam 20-30 minutes. Maintain water level; if too low, add more water.

ALFAJORES

Argentineans often enjoy alfajores, or lemon cookies, as an after-dinner snack and you can too.

- 1 Cup of sugar
- 1/2 Cup of butter
- 1 egg
- 2 egg yolks
- 2 teaspoons of grated lemon rind
- 1 teaspoon of vanilla
- 1/2 Cup of flour
- 1 1/2 Cup of cornstarch
- 1 teaspoon of baking powder

Cream the butter, add the sugar, and beat until fluffy. Add the egg and yolks, beat well, and then mix in the lemon rind and vanilla. In a separate bowl, combine the last three ingredients, pour them into the egg mixture, and stir well. On a greased cookie sheet, drop spoonfuls of the batter,
an inch apart. Preheat the oven to 350° and bake the cookies for 15 minutes; do not overcook. Let the cookies cool, eat them alone, or make a sandwich with dulce de leche, or sweet milk.

CHIMICHURRI SAUCE

This sauce is often served with beef, fish, or chicken. You can also use it as a marinade for your meat ahead of time and then grill.2 cups fresh parsley and/or cilantro

- 3-4 cloves of garlic
- 1/2 onion
- 1/2 Cup olive oil
- salt and pepper to taste

In a blender or food processor, add garlic, onion, fresh parsley, olive oil and a pinch of salt and pepper. Briefly blend 10-20 seconds. You want your mixture to be finely chopped but not pureed.

ARROZ BRANCO

Arroz Branco, or Brazilian style rice, requires few ingredients and little time. Start by getting:
- 1 Cup of rice
- 1 clove of garlic, minced
- 1 Tablespoon of chopped or grated onion
- 1/4 Cup Chopped carrot
- 1/4 Cup chopped tomato
- 1 Tablespoon of oil
- 1- 1/2 Cups of boiling water or chicken broth

In a saucepan, sauté the garlic, onion, and tomato or carrot in the oil. Add the rice and stir-fry before pouring in the water. Let the water boil until some of it evaporates, cover the pan, and reduce the flame. Once the rice is cooked, let it sit for ten minutes. Put it in a bowl and serve it with beans, sauce, or as a side dish.

Mexico

When we think of Mexican cooking; tacos are first on our mind. However Mexican recipes are much more diverse than that. Next time you want to have a Mexican taco try changing it a bit by adding different fillings such as fish, turkey, or chicken. Shredded pork tacos, black bean tacos or shrimp and avocado are all Mexican cooking at its best. Some common ingredients in Mexican food are lime juice, corn, cornmeal, flour tortillas, chili peppers, papaya, avocado, pineapple, and beans.

MEXICAN FOOD FACTS
• Corn is the major food grown in Mexico
• Mexico is famous for ice sherbets and drinks such as prickly pear cactus
• Authentic Mexican and North American Mexican type food is different

Kids Cooking Activities.com

MEXICO IS ALSO KNOWN FOR
- Mexico City is one of the largest cities in the world
- Mexico has many volcanoes
- Mexico has frequent earthquakes

LEARN A LITTLE LANGUAGE
- Comer con gusto means Enjoy the meal
- Buenos dias means good day
- Por Favor means Please

MEXICAN RECIPES

FLOUR TORTILLAS

These take a little muscle work to roll out, but they taste so good they are worth the extra effort.

- 4 Cups flour
- 2 teaspoons baking powder
- 2 teaspoons salt
- 4 Tablespoons oil
- 1 1/2 Cup warm water

In a mixing bowl add flour, baking powder and salt. Stir together. Pour in oil and warm water and blend together. Knead several minutes and let sit covered in plastic wrap or in a plastic container with a lid for 30 minutes. Pull off balls of dough and roll out each ball into desired size tortillas. Fry a few minutes on each side in a hot skillet. Prepare your favorite Mexican recipes with your fresh tortillas.

CHICKEN ENCHILADAS

- 2-3 Cups chopped cooked chicken
- 1 green pepper chopped, optional
- Chopped olives, optional
- Salsa
- 8 flour tortillas
- Cheddar cheese
- 1-2 cans red enchilada sauce
- 1 Cup sour cream

Place chopped cooked chicken in bowl. Stir in shredded cheddar cheese (as much as desired) chopped peppers or chopped olives. Sprinkle with salt and pepper and stir together. Spoon chicken mixture down the center of each tortilla, roll up. Place seam side down in baking dish. Top with enchilada sauce and sprinkle with cheddar cheese. Bake at 375 degrees for 20-25 minutes.

CHEESE QUESADILLAS
- 1 Cup shredded Mexican or Monterey Jack cheese
- 1 green onion, minced
- 1 Tablespoon canned chopped green chilies, corn and/or beans
- 4 8-inch flour tortillas

Mix cheese, onion, and chilies. On top of one flour tortilla scatter mix to the edges. Top with second tortilla. Brush tops with olive oil and bake in the oven at 400 degrees until golden brown. Or fry in a tablespoon of oil in a skillet. Top with sour cream, salsa, or tomatoes. **Make this a chicken quesadilla by adding chopped seasoned chicken with the cheese.

FAJITAS
- 2 Tablespoons lime juice
- 3 Tablespoons olive oil
- 1/2 teaspoon paprika
- 1 teaspoons chili powder
- 2 garlic cloves, minced
- 1 lb. chicken, or steak, cut into strips
- 1 onion, sliced
- 1 red or green bell pepper, cut into strips
- Flour tortillas
- Guacamole
- Salsa

Add lime juice, olive oil, paprika, chili powder and garlic in a plastic Ziploc bag or bowl. Add meat cut in strips and allow to marinate 3-4 hours. In skillet add contents of marinade (meat and liquid). Cook several minutes, add in onion slices, and pepper strips. Cook until vegetables are
tender and meat is cooked through. Serve fajita on a warm tortilla shell and top with guacamole and salsa if desired.

TAQUITOS
- 1 lb. ground beef
- 1 chopped onion
- 1 clove garlic, minced
- 1 Cup salsa
- 2 teaspoons chili powder
- 1/2 teaspoon salt
- 1/4 teaspoon pepper

Brown beef with chopped onion and garlic, minced. Drain and add salsa, chili powder, if desired, salt, and pepper.
Warm up flour tortillas and place beef mixture and shredded cheese on one end of tortilla. Wrap up tightly and place on a foil lined cookie sheet. When all tortillas are filled and rolled up brush tops of tortillas with oil. Bake at 400 degrees for 8-10 minutes or until golden brown. Serve with guacamole, sour cream and/or salsa.

GUACAMOLE
- 2 avocados
- 1 Tablespoon lemon juice
- 1/2 chopped tomato or desired amount of salsa
- 1/4 teaspoon salt
- 1/4 Cup sour cream, if desired.
Mash avocados and add remaining ingredients. Serve with tortilla chips.

SALSA
- Cut up tomatoes diced
- Onions however much you want
- One can mild green chilies
- 1-2 Garlic cloves, according to taste
- Salt to taste
Use as many ingredients as desired and taste as you go for a quick salsa.

EMPANADAS

- 1 1/2 Cup flour
- 1 Cup cornmeal
- 1 teaspoon baking powder
- 1/4 teaspoon salt
- 1 teaspoon sugar
- 1/3 Cup butter, softened
- 1/2 Cup milk
- 1 lb. ground beef
- 1 onion chopped
- 1/2 Cup shredded cheese

Brown hamburger and onion together in skillet. Season with salt and pepper or taco seasoning if you choose. Drain and set aside. Heat oven to 400. In a mixing bowl add flour, cornmeal, baking powder, salt, and sugar. Stir together and add soft butter. Blend together. Slowly add milk until dough forms a ball. If dough is sticky add more cornmeal. On a floured surface roll out dough and cut 3-4-inch circles with a bottom of a glass or biscuit cutter.

Add cheese to the beef mixture. Place 1 teaspoon of beef in each circle. Fold each circle in half and seal edges with a fork. Place on a cookie sheet and bake for 12 minutes or until golden brown. This recipe is very versatile as you can add whatever fillings you desire to change the recipe. Try ham and cheese, pizza toppings or a fruit filling for a non-Mexican empanada.

CORN AND TOMATO SIDE DISH
• 1 can of corn, drained
• 1-2 tomatoes, diced
• 1 avocado diced
• 2 Tablespoons olive oil
• 1 Tablespoon lime juice
• 1/4 Cup cilantro
• 1/4 teaspoon salt
• 1/4 teaspoon pepper
• diced red onion, optional

In serving bowl add corn, tomatoes, avocado, and onion. In measuring cup or bowl add olive oil, lime juice, cilantro, salt, and pepper together. Pour over salad and toss to coat. Serve immediately.

MEXICAN BEAN DIP
• 16 oz. refried beans mixed with ground beef
• Guacamole, homemade or store bought
• 1 Cup sour cream whisked together with taco seasoning mix
• Shredded lettuce
• Grated cheddar cheese
• Chopped tomatoes
• Chopped olives
• Chopped onions (optional)

Layer in each ingredient in order listed. Serve with tortilla chips.

Kids Cooking Activities.com

CHURROS
- 1/2 Cup water
- 2 Tablespoons butter or margarine
- pinch of sugar
- 6 Tablespoons flour
- 1 egg yolk
- 2 whole eggs
- Oil for frying
- Powdered sugar

In saucepan heat water, butter and sugar until butter has melted and sugar is dissolved. Add flour and blend together. Turn heat to low and cook continuing to stir until mixture forms a ball. It will be dry enough to leave the pan clean. In a small bowl whisk together eggs and egg yolk. Take off heat and slowly stir in beaten eggs. Allow to cool and then place in a Ziploc bag or pastry bag. (Clip a hole at the corner if using a Ziploc bag). Squeeze dough out into long sticks. Fry in hot oil until golden brown and crisp. Place on paper towel to drain. Then sprinkle with powdered sugar.

BAKED NOT FRIED ICE CREAM

It is still unsure if this is an ethnic Mexican cooking.
• 3 Cups cornflakes, crushed
• Vanilla ice cream

Place cornflakes in a Ziploc bag and crush with a rolling pin or kitchen mallet. Scoop vanilla ice cream in small scoops and roll in a ball. Coat with cereal. Place on a cookie sheet lined with waxed paper. Freeze several hours. Before serving broil for 30 seconds to until the cornflakes are light
brown.

Middle East

Middle Eastern Cooking covers many countries including Algeria, Bahrain, Egypt, Iraq, Iran, Israel, Jordan, Kuwait, Lebanon, Libya, Morocco, Oman, Palestine, Qatar, Saudi Arabia, Syria, Tunisia, Turkey, United Arab Emirates, and Yemen.

Some common Middle Eastern cooking ingredients include pita bread, lamb, eggplant, cumin, and cayenne pepper.

FOOD FACTS ABOUT MIDDLE EAST

• Saffron is a very expensive herb sold in Middle east selling $500-1000 per pound
• Pita bread is one of the oldest types of bread in the world

MIDDLE EAST IS ALSO KNOWN FOR SEVERAL FAMOUS THINGS:

• Gold
• Handmade carpets
• Warm tropical weather

LEARN A LITTLE LANGUAGE

• In Turkish, dinner means Akþam yemeði pronounced ak-sham ye-me-ee
• Thank you in Arabic - Shoo kran

MIDDLE EASTERN RECIPES

BABA GHANOUSH

- 1 medium eggplant
- 1 teaspoon olive oil
- 1/2 Cup onions minced
- 3 cloves garlic
- 1/4 Cup lemon juice
- 3 Tablespoons creamy peanut butter
- 1 Tablespoon fresh parsley minced
- 1/2 teaspoon black pepper

Preheat oven to 400. Pierce eggplant in several places with a fork. Place on cookie sheet lined with tin foil. Bake for 1 hour. Eggplant will be soft and flat. Allow to cool, then scoop out flesh into a blender. Discard skin. In skillet, heat oil and sauté onions and garlic. Cook and stir 3 minutes or until onions are transparent. Add to blender, add lemon juice, and peanut butter. Blend until smooth. Stir in parsley and pepper. Serve with toasted pita wedges, cooked chicken or cut vegetables.

TABBOULEH

- 1 head romaine lettuce
- 1 bunch parsley
- 1/2 Cup bulgur wheat
- 1/2 Cup boiling water
- 1 large tomato, finely diced
- 1 medium onion, minced
- 1 large cucumber, peeled, diced
- 1/2 Cup lemon juice
- 1/4 Cup vegetable oil
- Salt and pepper

Rinse and dry lettuce and parsley. Wrap parsley into a lettuce leave and chop lettuce and parsley in very small pieces. Set aside. Soak ½ Cup bulgur wheat in boiling water for about 30 minutes. Water will be completely absorbed by wheat. Add finely diced tomato, onion, and cucumber to bulgur after done soaking.

Stir in lettuce. Pour lemon juice and vegetable oil over mixture and toss to coat. Season with salt and pepper and serve recipe immediately.

*The key to this recipe is to chop vegetables finely.

MANTI

Manti is a Turkish dish.
• 1 package meat filled ravioli -homemade, frozen, or fresh
Sauce:
• 1 Cup plain yogurt
• Pinch of salt
• 1 teaspoon Parsley
• 3 cloves of garlic, minced
• 2 Tablespoons melted butter

Boil 8 quarts water. Gently add pasta to boiling water and simmer under reduced heat for 5 minutes or until ravioli rise to the top. Taste pasta for doneness. Mix sauce ingredients together and pour over cooked pasta squares. Serve immediately.

Kids Cooking Activities.com

FALAFEL

Falafels are fried balls or patties made from chick peas.

• 1 lb. chick peas, soaked overnight, cooked, and drained or 1 1/2 cans garbanzo beans
• 2 garlic cloves, minced
• 2 Tablespoons baking powder
• 1 teaspoon cumin ground
• 1 Tablespoon parsley
• 1 onion grated
• 1/2 Cup water
• 1/2 Cup flour
• Pinch of black pepper
• Oil for frying
• 1 tomato, sliced

Wash chickpeas and soak overnight in a large bowl. Drain chickpeas and add to a blender or food processor. Add chopped or grated onion and parsley. Blend together then add baking soda, salt, cumin, and pepper. Blend together again. Add ½ Cup water and 1/2 Cup flour to make a smooth paste. If mixture is still sticky add an additional tablespoon of flour and use wet hands to form into patties or balls. Or drop spoonfuls of dough into hot oil. Fry patties until browned on both sides. Serve warm with tomato slices and tahini sauce.

TAHINI SAUCE
- 2/3 Cup tahini (sesame paste)
- 3 Tablespoons water (or as needed)
- 2 lemons, juiced
- 2 garlic cloves, minced
- 1 Tablespoons fresh parsley, minced

Mix all ingredients together making a smooth sauce. Set aside.

HUMMUS
- 15 oz. can of garbanzo beans
- 1 garlic clove, chopped
- 1 teaspoon salt
- 1/4 Cup cold water
- 5 Tablespoons lemon juice
- 1/3 Cup tahini paste

Open beans with can opener and drain liquid out. Place beans in a bowl and mash with a potato masher or use the food processor. Stir in garlic clove, salt, cold water, lemon juice and tahini paste. Eat with pita bread.

YOGURT SOUP

- 8 Cups chicken broth
- 2/3 Cup flour
- 1 Cup rice
- 3 Cups plain yogurt
- 2 eggs
- 2 Tablespoons butter
- 2 Tablespoons mint *

Boil rice in 8 Cups chicken broth on low heat until rice is done. Whip flour, yogurt, and eggs together until smooth. Add into the boiling chicken broth. Stir until well blended. Melt butter in saucepan and add mint. Sauté for one minute and stir mint into soup.

* Mint is used in many dishes in Middle Eastern cooking. In this dish it is especially essential with the yogurt.

LABNEH

A recipe that is often served with bread for breakfast.
- 3 Cups plain yogurt
- 1 teaspoon salt

Prepare this one day before using. In bowl stir yogurt and salt together. Place on top of a large piece of cheesecloth. Tie up ends together, place a bowl under the cheesecloth to catch drips and hang in the fridge for 12-24 hours. The next day you should have a creamy sauce like sour cream or cream cheese.

TURKISH KOFTA

- 1 Cup fine fresh breadcrumbs
- 1 lb. lean ground lamb
- 1/2 teaspoon salt
- 1/2 teaspoon pepper
- 1 teaspoon ground cumin
- 1/2 teaspoon allspice
- 1 teaspoon dried mint
- 2 cloves garlic
- 2 Tablespoons parsley
- 1 egg
- 1 Tablespoon olive oil

Add ingredients together (except olive oil) in a large bowl. Knead ingredients together with your hands several minutes. Shape into balls or sausage shapes and grill or bake in olive oil. These can be served in pita bread with tomatoes, cucumbers, and hummus. You may substitute ground pork or ground beef for the lamb.

Morocco

Moroccan food recipes are becoming popular throughout the world. Morocco is known for tagines, mint tea, camel rides in the dessert and warm beautiful weather. Learn a little about the kingdom of Morocco and try some ethnic Moroccan recipes.

COMMON MOROCCAN INGREDIENTS
• Spices such as cinnamon, cloves, turmeric, cumin, ginger, saffron
• lamb or sheep meat
• eggplants
• tomatoes
• lemon juice

Kids Cooking Activities.com

- mint
- couscous
- garbanzo beans
- olives
- fresh fruits such as dates, figs, pomegranates, oranges, lemons, apricots, plums

MOROCCAN FACTS
- Morocco is located in the Northwest corner of Africa.
- If you travel to the farthest tip North, you can see the Rock of Gibraltar across the sea.
- Lions and elephants lived in Morocco but not anymore. Now you will find geckos, lizards, chameleons, and snakes. As well as camels, sheep
and Barbary monkeys
- Morocco is a kingdom.
- Part of the Sahara Dessert can be found in Morocco and taking a camel trek through the desert is a big tourist destination.

LEARN A LITTLE LANGUAGE
- Inshallah- means God willing or if God wills it to be. (Arabic)
- Shukran - Thank you (Arabic)
- Mange- eat (French)

MOROCCON RECIPES

ZAALOUK- EGGPLANT SALAD

- 2 eggplants
- 3-4 tomatoes, fresh
- dash pepper
- salt to taste
- 1 Tablespoon paprika
- 1 teaspoon cumin
- 4 garlic cloves
- 1/4-1/2 Cup olive oil

Wash and poke the eggplants several places with a fork or knife. Place on a cookie sheet and let roast at 400 degrees F/200 C for 1 hour. Allow to cool. Another variation is to peel you eggplant and cut in cubes. Boil in salted water for 30 minutes. If roasted eggplant, peel off skin off and discard. Chop eggplants and tomatoes in small pieces. Place in a saucepan. Drizzle with oil and season with pepper, paprika, cumin salt and add minced garlic. Allow to cook and sauté 10-20 minutes. Taste and season more if needed. Traditionally, this is served with slices of fresh loaf bread or pita bread.

CHICKEN TANGINE

Tagines are famous dishes usually cooked meat with vegetables and spices. It is cooked in a tagine dish or pot. It is usually cooked on top of the stove but can also be used on a campfire or inside the oven.

• 1/4 Cup butter
• 1/2 teaspoon ginger
• season with salt and pepper
• 1/4 teaspoon ground cinnamon
• 1/4 teaspoon cumin
• 1 large onion, grated
• 1 lb. chicken breasts or cut up chicken
• 1/2 - 1 1/2 Cups water

• sliced and peeled vegetables such as potatoes, carrots, parsnips, etc.

In your tagine pot, Dutch oven or large soup pan melt 1/4 Cup butter and sauté your onion. Add in ginger, salt, pepper, cinnamon, and cumin. Blend spices into the onion and butter. Add chicken pieces on top of the melted butter. Cook for 10 minutes then add 1/2- 1 Cup water, enough to cover the meat. Add chopped potatoes, zucchini, or other vegetables you would like on top of the chicken. Put lid on and cook for 40 minutes.

Kids Cooking Activities.com

HARIRA

This soup recipe is served during the holy month of Ramadan.
- 3-4 tomatoes
- 1 onion chopped or grated
- 2 Tablespoons butter
- 1/2 Cup fresh parsley, chopped
- 2 Tablespoons tomato paste
- 4 teaspoons salt
- 1 teaspoon ginger
- several dashes pepper
- 1/2 teaspoon cumin
- 2 Cups garbanzo beans, soaked overnight and cooked until tender or 1 can drained
- 1/2 Cup dried lentils, soaked in water for 30 minutes-1 hour
- 1/3 Cup rice
- 8 Cups water
- 1/3 Cup flour

Puree tomatoes in a blender. In a soup pot sauté onions in the butter. Stir in pureed tomatoes, chopped parsley, lentils, garbanzo beans, salt, pepper, ginger, cumin, and water. Allow to cook for 30-40 minutes. Stir in tomato paste and rice. Allow to cook until rice is tender.

*To thicken your soup, take out a 1/4 Cup of soup and add flour a little at a time. Whisk until smooth. Blend into soup and allow to cook until soup thickens.

New England USA

Of all the New England recipes, the most popular has to be clam chowder, as dinners and restaurants throughout the United States serve it on a daily basis. Boston cream pie, Maine lobsters, Johnny Cakes, and baked beans are just as noteworthy when exploring recipes of America's Northeastern region. For over 400 years, people have been perfecting and passing down these and other traditional regional recipes native to New England.

COMMON NEW ENGLAND INGREDIENTS

- Fish, clams, lobsters
- Blueberries
- Cranberries
- Corn
- Beans
- Maple syrup
- Yams
- Ham
- Sweet relish

FACTS ABOUT NEW ENGLAND

- New England was one of the earliest settlements in the USA. Where the pilgrims from the Mayflower first settled.
- The region is made up of six diverse USA states: Connecticut, Maine, Massachusetts, New Hampshire, Rhode Island, and Vermont.
- Many family farms in this area provide fresh produce
- This area has many outdoor adventures such as fishing, mountain hiking, skiing
- Cranberries and blueberries grow wild in this region of the USA

NEW ENGLAND RECIPES

RHODE ISLAND'S JOHNNY CAKE

The Johnny Cake has been around since 1796; at least that's when the first recipe was documented. Also known as the hoecake, Indian slapjack, corn pone, and batter bread, it started in Rhode Island but also has roots in America's southern and mid-western states. Varieties of sweet and unsweetened New England recipes are available to make this simple dish, but the following is the one originally used over 200 years ago.

To make unsweetened Johnny Cakes, you need:
• 1 Cup of white cornmeal
• 1/4 Cup of flour
• 1/2 Cup milk.
For **sweet Johnny Cakes**, add:
• 1 Tablespoon molasses
• 1/2 Cup shortening
• 1 Cup cold water
• 3/4 teaspoon salt

Combine the ingredients for whichever cake you prefer, mold them into small flat cakes, and cook them on low heat in a greased pan like a pancake. When the first side is light brown, flip it over and lightly brown the other side. Enjoy this meal for breakfast, as a snack, or a side dish.

SUCCOTASH
- 1- 10 oz. package of frozen corn or 2 cans corn, drained
- 2 cans lima beans, drained or 2 Cups cooked lima beans- if you prefer kidney beans or other beans you can substitute them for lima beans
- salt and pepper to taste
- 1 Tablespoon butter

This simple dish can be prepared in the microwave or on the stovetop. Add corn, beans and butter into a microwave safe dish or saucepan. Sprinkle with salt and pepper and stir to combine. Cook several minutes until corn and beans are warmed and butter is melted. Stir butter to combine and serve.

Kids Cooking Activities.com

BOSTON'S BAKED BEANS

Boston baked beans are one of the New England recipes loaded with sugar, fat, and a whole lot of flavor, so while you may not want to eat them every day, you are going to want to eat them occasionally.

- 2 lbs. yellow eye beans
- 1/4 lb. chopped bacon
- 1 teaspoon each of salt, dry mustard, baking soda, and powdered ginger
- pinch black pepper
- 1/2 Cup each of dark brown sugar and dark molasses
- 1 Cup maple syrup
- 4 Cups chicken broth

Preheat your oven to 325° and boil the beans with the baking soda in an eight-quart pot for three to five minutes. Rinse the beans, put fresh water in the pot, and cook for an additional 30 minutes or until the skins split. Drain and rinse with cold water. Put the beans back in the pot, add the bacon, broth, and spices, and simmer until the beans are soft.

Pour in the sugar, molasses, syrup, and remove from the stove. Put the mixture into a three-quart greased baking dish, cover it, and cook for an hour or two, until

the beans are brown. Occasionally stir the mixture and add water or broth so that the beans stay moist. When it's done, let it cool, scoop it up, and serve this staple among New England recipes as a side dish.

CLAM CHOWDER

The most famous of all New England recipes, clam chowder stems from Cape Cod and is a hearty dish that warms winter bellies.

- 8 lbs. clean quahog clams
- 4 pieces of bacon, chopped
- 1-2 onions, diced finely or grated
- 1 Cup of chopped celery
- 3 Tablespoons of butter
- 2-3 cloves garlic, minced
- 2 bay leaves
- 1 teaspoon dried thyme
- 2 Cups heavy cream
- 4-5 potatoes, peeled and diced
- pinch of salt and pepper

Bring two cups of water to a boil, add the clams, cover, and cook for five minutes before stirring. Cook five to ten minutes more or until the clams open. Pour the broth into a bowl using a strainer so that it equals six cups; if it's less, add more water. Chop the clams into smaller pieces and set aside.

Cook the bacon in a large pot until it's crispy, dispose of the fat, add the onions, butter, and celery; cook until tender. Add the garlic, bay leaves, and thyme, then cook three minutes; don't brown. Pour in the clam broth and potatoes, boil, reduce the heat, cover, and simmer for a half hour or until the broth thickens and the potatoes are soft. Remove the pot from the stove, stir in the heavy cream and clams, season, and let sit covered for one hour.

Put the pot back on the stove and slowly reheat the chowder without boiling. Serve with rolls or crackers and enjoy delicious New England cooking.

Russia

Russian food recipes can vary by region and the people who live in those regions. Wherever the recipe originated it is sure to offer a taste of the country and its people. Many Russians make large quantities because traditionally the Russian people's lives are centered around their families and family gatherings.

COMMON RUSSIAN INGREDIENTS

- wheat
- rye
- millet
- barley
- fish
- chicken
- mushrooms
- smoked meats
- caviar
- potatoes
- carrots
- turnips
- green onions

145

- dill
- cucumbers
- mustard
- garlic
- horseradish

FACTS ABOUT RUSSIA
- Russia is the largest country in the world
- Siberia covers 3/4 of Russia
- Home to 100,000 rivers
- Siberian tigers roam the forests of Eastern Russia
- Russia has many famous authors, artists, and ballerinas
- Lake Baikal has the most water compared to other lakes throughout the world
- Only about 10% of Russia's land can be used for farming because of the cold climate
- Hockey, soccer, and chess are major pastimes

LEARN A LITTLE LANGUAGE
- Babushkas- Grandmothers
- Spasiba - thank you
- Privet - hello
- Prijatnovo appetita- Bon appetit

RUSSIAN FOOD RECIPES
Russians grows over 40 million tons of wheat a year. Wheat pancakes, called blini are one of this country's favorite foods and they are not just for breakfast. Blini (BLEE-nee) are so popular in Russia that there are festivals centered around them.
They are especially popular with the Slavic people, who live in the plain's regions of the country. The round golden shape food symbolizes the sun. They are featured at spring festivals that mark the end of winter and the beginning of the wheat growing season.

BLINI OR BUCKWHEAT PANCAKE RECIPE

- 1 egg
- 2 Tablespoons melted butter
- 1 Cup milk
- 1 teaspoon instant yeast
- 2/3 Cup all-purpose flour
- 1/2 Cup buckwheat flour
- Pinch of salt

Mix flours, yeast, and salt in a large bowl. Make a well in the center of the mixture. Add milk and mix until batter becomes smooth. Cover and let rise for 1 hour. Melt butter, add egg yolk, and stir into the batter. Beat the egg white, in a small bowl until stiff. Add this to the batter, cover and let stand for 15-20 minutes. Heat a non-stick skillet over medium low to medium heat. Drop teaspoon size mounds of dough into skillet. Cook until bubbly around the edges or about one minute. Flip over and cook for another 30 seconds. Repeat until all dough is used. Will make 20-24 blini.

Once your blini is prepared there are a number of toppings that can be added to the blini to turn them into a meal. For a **breakfast blini**, butter, jam, or a hardboiled egg are often the toppings of choice.

To turn a blini into a heartier meal, **for lunch or dinner,** Russians may add cream cheese, smoked salmon, or lox. Maybe even a small slice of brie with sliced grapes. Blinis are also popular fare in more elegant settings. As an **appetizer** at a dinner party, they may be topped with sour cream, caviar, or honey with soft fruits, like a sliced strawberry. They are often served at weddings and receptions as well.

Here is a quick recipe for a unique topping:

- one 16 oz. block of cream cheese, softened
- 6 slices bacon
- 3-5 green onions

Fry bacon until crisp. Wrap between two paper towels and blot excess grease. Set aside Wash green onions, dry, and chop finely.

Kids Cooking Activities.com

Put softened cream cheese in medium mixing bowl. Crumble bacon into cream cheese and mix thoroughly. Mix green onions into cream cheese and bacon mixture or if you prefer, sprinkle lightly on top of mixture after it has been spread on blini. Spread mixture thinly on blini and ENJOY!

RUSSIAN EASTER BREAD

This traditional Russian Easter Bread recipe could also be called Babka, meaning sweet yeast cake. In Bulgaria it is called Kozunak. Russian's call it Kulich.

• 1 Cup milk, warm
• 1 Tablespoon or 1 pkg. Yeast
• 1 Tablespoon sugar
• 1/2 Cup warm water
• 2 eggs
• 10 egg yolks
• 3/4 Cup butter, melted
• 2 teaspoons vanilla extract
• 1/2 Cup sugar
• 2 teaspoons lemon zest about 2 lemons
• juice from one lemon
• 3/4 Cup raisins
• 5 1/2-6 Cups flour

Warm milk and pour into mixing bowl. Warm water and add sugar and yeast. Set aside and let dissolve. In mixing bowl, add 2 eggs and egg yolks. Save some egg whites in the fridge for brushing on the top later. Melt butter and add to bowl. Rub the outside of your lemons with a small grater and add to mixing bowl. Add in vanilla, sugar, and lemon juice. Blend all together. Add in 2 Cups flour and yeast mixture. Blend together. Add raisins and remaining flour to make a nice soft ball. Add dough to a floured surface and knead several minutes. Knead in raisins. Place a tablespoon of oil in a large clean bowl and add your dough.

Cover with a towel and let rise 1 hour. Punch down and rise another 30 minutes. Shape dough into loaves if making loaves or shape into a braid, rolls, whatever you'd like. In a typical Russian Easter Bread recipe, the dough is often placed in clean coffee cans or gallon cans at this point, filling about 1/2 full. Cover your dough and let rise another 30 minutes.

Take out the egg whites you saved before and add 2 Tablespoons water. Sprinkle with sugar. Brush tops of your dough and bake at 350 degrees until golden brown. Time will vary as to the size and shape of your bread.

BEET SALAD

- 4 beets
- 4 garlic cloves, minced
- 1/2 Cup black walnuts, chopped finely
- 1/4 Cup mayonnaise
- 1/4 Cup or less honey
- pinch of salt

Wash and place beets on cookie sheet. Roast beets in the oven at 400 degrees for 30-50 minutes until a fork can pierce through the skin. Allow to cool. Peel skin off and grate beets into a serving dish. Add in minced garlic, chopped walnuts, mayonnaise, and honey. Stir until well combined. Serve immediately or store in the fridge until ready to serve.

See more Russian food recipes such as Borscht on our Eastern European cooking pages.

South Africa

Thanks to my good friend Wendy Young from South Africa who put this page together. You can visit her site at South African Homeschool Curriculum. http://www.south-african-homeschool-curriculum.
com/

South African recipes are influenced by the country's mixture of people, languages, and culture groups. The food is indicative of this mix and has produced a wide range of tastes and techniques. The bulk of the Black African people today live a westernized lifestyle but in the traditional black

villages in the rural areas of South Africa the staple diet is vegetable and mielie pap. Mielie pap is a maize meal porridge often served with gravy and a little meat if available. Samp and beans is another traditional meal.

The first white inhabitants in South Africa were primarily three groups: Dutch, French and British. The food that comes from the descendants of the Dutch makes up the typical "Boere Kos" (Farmers Food) that is still enjoyed by many. Another large group of people particularly in the Western Cape are the Cape Malay people who originate from the earliest slaves in the Cape. Their curries are renowned all over the country.

Kids Cooking Activities.com

MUTTON CURRY

This is a quick and easy choice, in our Cape Malay recipes. Mutton being a tougher meat needs a little longer to cook, though.

- 1.5 kg/3 lbs. boneless mutton shoulder
- Oil
- 4 onions, chopped
- 15 ml/ 1 Tablespoon curry powder
- 5 ml/1 teaspoon turmeric
- 10 ml/2 teaspoons salt
- 2 ml/1/2 teaspoon black pepper
- 1 stick cinnamon
- 3 cloves
- 2 bay leaves
- 2 carrots
- 250 grams/1/2 lb. Apricots
- 2 bananas, sliced
- 125 ml/ 1/2 Cup wine vinegar
- 500ml/ 2 Cups meat stock

Cut meat into cubes, fry in oil until brown. Add onions and sauté. Add curry powder and turmeric, fry lightly. Add all remaining seasonings, then carrots and fruit. Add vinegar and stock, cook until meat is tender, 2–3 hours. Serve with yellow rice.

Southern United States

Southern Cooking in the United States covers many types of food such as soul food, Creole cooking/Cajun, and barbecue. In Florida you will hear of the popular Key Lime Pie whereas Texas is known for great steaks and chili.

FOOD FACTS ABOUT SOUTHERN USA

• Collard greens, turnips and okra are popular vegetables eaten in the Southern USA.
• Boiled peanuts are a favorite snack. Another name for these is goober peas.
• Biscuits with a milk gravy is a favorite breakfast food in the South.

SOME FAMOUS THINGS ABOUT THE SOUTHERN UNITED STATES

• Growing cotton, peanuts, pecans
• Coca Cola was invented in Georgia
• American Civil War
• Blues, Jazz, and Country music

Kids Cooking Activities.com

SOUTHERN USA RECIPES

FRIED CHICKEN
- 1-2 lbs. chicken pieces, cut up
- 2 Cups buttermilk
- 1 teaspoon black pepper
- 1/4 teaspoon salt
- 1 1/4 Cups flour
- 1 1/2 teaspoons seasoned salt
- 1 lb. vegetable
shortening or vegetable oil
- 1/2 Cup butter

Combine buttermilk, 1/4 teaspoon pepper, and salt. Add chicken pieces and refrigerate overnight. Combine flour, seasoned salt and 3/4 teaspoon pepper in baking dish. Heat shortening and butter in pan until it reaches 365 degrees on a thermometer. Take chicken out of buttermilk and coat in flour mixture. Fry until golden brown and cooked through.

CHEESE GRITS
- 2 Cups water
- 1/4 Cup quick cooking grits
- 1/4 Cup shredded cheddar cheese
- 1 Tablespoon butter
- 1 egg, separated
- 1/4 Cup milk

In a saucepan boil 2 cups water then stir in grits. Turn heat down and cover with a lid. Cook about 5 minutes. Stirring occasionally. After 5 minutes add butter and cheese. Separate egg yolk from egg white. Set aside egg white for later. In a small glass beat egg yolk with milk. Add to grits mixture. Stir to combine. In a mixing bowl whip egg white until stiff peaks form. Stir into grits. Pour grits into a greased casserole dish. Bake at 350 degrees for 1 hour. You can also add cooked crumbled sausage to the grits before baking.

156

Kids Cooking Activities.com

HOMEMADE MACARONI AND CHEESE
- 12 oz. pasta or macaroni
- 3 Tablespoons butter
- 3 Tablespoons flour
- 1 1/2 teaspoon mustard
- 1/4 teaspoon salt
- 2 Cups evaporated milk
- 3/4 teaspoon Tabasco sauce
- 2 Cups cheddar cheese, shredded
- 1 Cup Gouda cheese shredded
- 3/4 Cup Parmesan cheese

Cook pasta. Meanwhile, melt butter in saucepan. Stir in flour, mustard, and salt. Cook, whisking constantly. Mixture will thicken. Whisk in milk and Tabasco until mixture is smooth. Cook, until slightly thickened. Stir in 1 ½ Cup Cheddar, Gouda, and Parmesan cheese until smooth and melted. Stir in hot pasta. Stir to combine. Spoon mixture into baking dish. Sprinkle with remaining cheddar cheese. Broil until lightly browned. Serve immediately.

PECAN PIE
This southern cooking recipe uses pecans that grow in Texas.
- Pie crust for one-layer pie
- 2/3 Cup white sugar
- 1/3 Cup butter, melted
- 1 Cup corn syrup
- 1/2 teaspoon salt
- 3 large eggs
- 1 Cup pecans

Prepare pie crust for bottom of pie. Set aside and preheat the oven to 375 degrees. In mixing bowl blend sugar, melted butter, corn syrup, salt, and eggs together. Stir in pecans. Pour into prepared pie crust. Bake for 40-45 minutes until center is set.

BARBECUE BEEF

Barbecue beef or pork is famous in Southern Cooking and contests are often held to see who has the best barbecue recipe.
• Beef or pork roast
• 2 onions, chopped
• 1/2 Cup water

Place meat, onions and water in crock pot and cook 6-8 hours. Drain and set broth aside for later. Shred meat with a fork. Prepare barbecue sauce.

HOMEMADE BARBECUE SAUCE

• 3/4 Cup meat broth (broth you drained and set aside from above)
• 2 Cups ketchup
• 2 teaspoons mustard
• 2 Tablespoons vinegar
• 3 Tablespoons brown sugar
• 3 Tablespoons Worcestershire sauce
• 1/2 teaspoon liquid smoke
• Salt and pepper to taste

Combine all sauce ingredients in a bowl. Stir shredded meat into the sauce and pour back in the crockpot for about 20 minutes. Serve shredded meat on buns or rolls.

PEACH COBBLER

Peaches grow in Georgia making peach cobbler a common southern cooking recipe.

- 1/2 Cup sugar
- 1 Tablespoon cornstarch
- 1/4 teaspoon ground cinnamon
- 1/4 teaspoon nutmeg
- 4 Cups sliced peaches
- 1 teaspoon lemon juice
- 3 Tablespoons shortening
- 1 Cup all-purpose flour
- 1 Tablespoon sugar
- 1 1/2 teaspoons baking powder
- 1/2 teaspoon salt
- 1/2 teaspoon milk

In a mixing bowl blend together flour, 1 Tablespoon sugar, baking powder and salt. Mix until flour mixture resembles fine crumbs. Stir in ½ teaspoon milk and set aside. In saucepan mix ½ Cup sugar, cornstarch, cinnamon, and nutmeg together. Add peaches and lemon juice. Cook over medium heat and constantly stir until mixture thickens and comes to a boil. Allow to boil about 1-2 minutes. Pour into a small casserole dish. Spread flour mixture over the top of peaches. Bake at 400 degrees for 25 minutes or until golden brown.

NEW ORLEANS- CAJUN COOKING/ CREOLE COOKING

CAJUN CATFISH

- 1-pound catfish filets
- 1/4 Cup yellow cornmeal
- 1/4 Cup dry breadcrumbs
- 1 teaspoon chili powder
- 1/2 teaspoon paprika

If you have Cajun seasoning spice substitute that for the paprika and chili powder. In shallow dish or pie plate add cornmeal, breadcrumbs, and seasonings. You can also season with salt and pepper if desired. Cut catfish into small strips. Coat both sides of fish in cornmeal mixture. Place on cookie sheet or casserole dish and broil at 450 degrees for about 15 minutes until a fork inserted in the fish shows it is done. (It will be flaky)

JAMBALAYA

- 1 package polish kielbasa or sausage your family likes
- 1 1/2 cups uncooked rice
- 1 1/2 cups chicken broth
- 1/4 tsp dried thyme leaves
- 1/4 teaspoon chili powder
- Chopped green pepper
- 1 small onion, quartered
- 1 can chopped tomatoes, undrained

Cut sausage into slices. In large skillet cook sausage flipping over and browning each side. Set aside and wipe out grease from pan. Add uncooked rice, chicken broth, thyme, chili powder, chopped pepper, quartered onion, and chopped tomatoes with juice. Stir all together and add sausage back to the pan. Cover with a lid and simmer on medium about 10-15 minutes until rice is done.

**If desired, add quick cooking shrimp along with the southern cooking ingredients before simmering.

RED BEANS AND RICE SOUP
• 4 slices of bacon
• 2 celery stalks
• 1 leek
• 1 green bell pepper
• 2 cans red kidney beans, drained or equivalent to 2-3 cups
• 1 teaspoon thyme
• 1-2 bay leaves
• 6 Cups water
• 1 teaspoon salt
• 1/4 teaspoon pepper
• 2 Cups rice, cooked

Cook and chop bacon. Cut leek, celery, and bell pepper in small pieces. Combine vegetables, beans, thyme, and water in large pot. Cook covered on medium-low until vegetables are soft. Season with salt and pepper and stir in cooked rice. Top each serving with bacon pieces.

Southwest Recipes

American Southwest recipes are more than just BBQ and a taste of Mexico; they are unique, flavorful, and each state has its own special treats. Southwestern cuisine is a mixture of flavors and spices, influenced by the Spanish colonial settlers and Native American tribes as well as Mexican neighbors. Texas has its own version of huevos rancheros, a signature breakfast dish from Mexico, complete with chili, while college students at Arizona State University enjoy an original chicken dish dubbed "Club Pollo Santa Fe." Residents of New Mexico enjoy one of the more creative condiments, cactus jelly, for breakfast, lunch, or with dinner rolls.

COMMON SOUTHWESTERN INGREDIENTS

- corn
- black beans
- chilies
- cumin
- coriander
- cilantro
- agave
- figs
- mango
- pumpkin
- yucca
- tomatillo
- jicama
- blue corn
- cactus
- tortillas

FACTS ABOUT SOUTHWESTERN USA

• The Southwestern USA is considered to be Arizona, New Mexico, Oklahoma, and Texas

• Four Corners Monument is located in this area where states, Arizona, Colorado, New Mexico, and Utah, meet up in one spot.

• The Southwest has many monuments and national parks including the Grand Canyon.

SOUTHWESTERN RECIPES

TEX-MEX CHILE EGGS

People say breakfast is the most important meal of the day, so why not start your morning with Southwest recipes that call for chilies and eggs cooked Texas style. Gather up:

- 1/2 an onion and green pepper, chopped
- 4 cans of green chile peppers, chopped
- 4 cloves of garlic, cut small
- 1 can of diced tomatoes
- 2 corn tortillas
- 4 eggs
- Green enchilada sauce
- Fresh chopped cilantro
- Salt, black pepper, and red pepper

Turn your oven to 375° and cover a baking sheet with foil. Meanwhile, in a frying pan, sauté onions and green peppers in olive oil until they are tender. Add in the garlic, green chilies, tomatoes, salt, and peppers. Stir to combine and continue to cook several minutes until thickens. Pour into a serving dish. With a pastry brush, brush oil on both sides of the tortillas. Place on the baking sheets. Warm for a few minutes in the oven. Fry eggs in your skillet. To prepare your eggs, place a tortilla on a serving plate. Add a spoonful of prepared sauce. Place your cooked eggs on top and then add a spoonful of green chile sauce. Garnish with cilantro, sour cream, or anything else you like on your eggs and savor this Southwest recipes.

BLACK BEAN SOUP
• 1 teaspoon vegetable oil
• 2 garlic cloves, minced
• 2 Cups water
• 1/2 teaspoon chipotle chile powder
• 3 cans black beans, rinsed and drained
• 1- 8 oz. bottle salsa
• 1 tablespoon fresh lime juice

In a soup pan, sauté garlic in oil for 1 minute, stirring often. Add in water, chile powder, black beans, salsa, and lime juice. Cook 5-10 minutes until warmed through and serve with tortilla chips or topped with guacamole, sour cream and/or shredded cheddar cheese.

BLACK BEAN AND MANGO QUESADILLA
• 1 teaspoon olive oil
• 1 chopped or grated onion
• 1/2 teaspoon dried oregano
• pinch salt and pepper
• 1 poblano chile, seeded and chopped finely
• 1 (15 oz.) can black beans, rinsed and drained
• 1 mango sliced and chopped
• 1/3 Cup cubed peeled avocado
• Flour or corn tortillas
• 1/2 Cup sharp cheddar cheese

In a frying pan, sauté onion and chopped chile in oil. Stir in black beans and season with oregano, salt, and pepper. Warm for several minutes stirring to combine. Take off heat and add a spoonful of mixture to the top of a tortilla. Spread around. Add chopped mango, avocado, and sprinkle with cheese. Add another tortilla on the top. In frying pan, add quesadilla and fry until browned on both sides.

Kids Cooking Activities.com

ASU CLUB POLLO SANTA FE CHICKEN

Of the many Southwest recipes, this one is so popular it has made its way from the Arizona State University cafeteria, into homes.
- 4 thin, boneless chicken breasts
- 3 poblano and Anaheim peppers, roasted
- 1/4 Cup of onions, chopped
- 1/2 Cup of goat cheese crumbles
- 1 minced clove of garlic
- 1 Tablespoon garlic powder
- 1 Tablespoon red chili powder
- 1 Tablespoon cumin
- pinch of salt and pepper

In a small bowl blend together garlic powder, chili powder, salt, pepper, and cumin. This is called a dry rub. With your fingers rub the spice mixture over the chicken and place on a baking sheet.
Have an adult help chop hot peppers and wear plastic gloves, if needed. Sauté in a frying pan, peppers, onions, and garlic in a frying pan, with a small amount of oil.

When chicken is done baking serve the sautéed peppers and onions over the top of your chicken. Sprinkle goat cheese over the top and serve.

Spain

Spanish recipes are flavorful and should not be confused with Mexican or Latin American dishes, as they are quite different. Among some of the traditional Spanish dishes are gazpacho, paella, tapas, and sangria, as well as crema catalana and flan. From appetizers to drinks to desserts, Spanish cuisine offers a variety of tastes to tickle your palette and fill your belly.

COMMON SPANISH INGREDIENTS
- peppers
- olive oil
- garlic
- paprika
- ham
- fish and seafood
- cheese
- sausages or chorizo
- nuts
- chickpeas
- eggplant
- zucchini as well as other fresh fruit and vegetables

FACTS ABOUT SPAIN

• Bullfighting is considered an art in Spain and is still very popular today.
• Spain is the closest European country to the continent of Africa.
• Soccer is the most popular sport in Spain.
• Flamenco music and Spanish dancing is very popular in the western region.
• Stores close around 1 pm for an afternoon siesta
• Spain is one of the most mountainous countries in Europe
• Spain has over 4,000 miles of beaches

LEARN A LITTLE LANGUAGE

• Hello- Hola
• Good morning - buenas días
• Thank you very much - muchas gracias
• I'm Hungry– tengo hambre

SPAIN RECIPES

TAPAS

In Spain, appetizers, or tapas, replace the main course, as you would order a variety of items instead of a meal. This is an interesting and fun way to eat because it allows you the opportunity to try new things, share a portion of your dish, and taste a little of everything. Some popular tapas dishes are foie toast with jamon, or ham, shrimp fritters, and stuffed tomatoes. Another common item found on the tapas menu is pimientos rellenos, or rice-stuffed peppers.

GAZPACHO

• 2 tomatoes, cut in fourths or 2 cups canned tomatoes
• 1 cucumber peeled and cut in pieces
• 1/2 small onion, peeled and sliced
• 1 green pepper, remove seeds and cut in slices
• 3 Cups tomato juice
• 1/3 Cup white or red wine vinegar
• 1/4 Cup olive oil
• 1 teaspoon salt
• 1/4 teaspoon pepper

Add all ingredients to blender and blend. Serve with chopped cucumbers, tomatoes, green peppers, or croutons if desired.

PAELLA

- Olive oil
- Onion, chopped
- 2 cloves garlic, minced
- 2 Tablespoons of chicken bouillon
- 3 chicken breasts, cubed
- 2 green peppers, chopped
- 1 red pepper, chopped
- 8 oz. tomato sauce
- 4 Cups of rice
- 7 Cups of water
- Pinch of salt
- 1/2 lb.- 1 lb. shrimp
- 1 lb. scallops

In frying pan sauté onion and garlic. Stir chicken bouillon into onion and garlic. Add chopped chicken and diced peppers. Cook until chicken is no longer pink. Stir in tomato sauce. Add rice and water and bring to a boil. Sprinkle with salt and pepper. Boil 5-7 minutes then add in shrimp and scallops. Boil and simmer 10 minutes. If needed add a little more water.

Kids Cooking Activities.com

TORTILLA DE PATATAS

- 3/4 Cup-1 Cup olive oil
- 4 potatoes peeled and cut very thin
- Salt and pepper
- 1 onion, thinly sliced
- 4 eggs

Add olive oil to a frying pan. Add potato and onion slices layering the bottom of the pan. Cook over medium-low. You just want to cook them slowly and not make the potatoes crispy. Meanwhile in large bowl add 4 eggs and beat together. Sprinkle with salt and pepper. With a slotted spoon take potatoes and onions out of oil in frying pan. Add to your bowl of eggs.
Potatoes should soak in the eggs 10-15 minutes Heat oil in pan again. If needed add more oil. Add potatoes and eggs and allow to cook without stirring. You can use your spatula to move around the edges, but you want to let the eggs set like you were making an omelet. When potatoes start to get crispy, place a large lid, plate, or cookie sheet on the top of your pan.

Flip potatoes onto lid. Place back in frying pan cooking opposite side. Continue to cook until both sides are done.

RICE STUFFED PEPPERS

- 1 lb. of short grain Spanish Rice
- 5 colored bell peppers, one of which you must chop
- 1/2 onion, chopped
- 2-3 Tablespoons of olive oil
- 1/2 tomato, skinned and chopped
- 5 oz. chopped pork
- Fresh parsley, chopped
- Saffron
- Salt

Begin by cutting the stems off the peppers and cleaning out the insides. Next, heat the oil and sauté the chopped red pepper until it is tender.

Remove it from the heat, then fry the onion until it is soft. Add the pork, brown it, put in the tomato, the cooked pepper, the uncooked rice, saffron, parsley, and salt to taste. Stuff the remaining peppers and lay them in a baking dish so that the filling does not come out. Cover the peppers and cook them for an hour and a half.

More International Recipes

NATIVE AMERICAN
FRY BREAD TACOS
• Bread dough
• Chili
• Ground beef, cooked
• Shredded cheese
• Taco fixings

With your bread dough, form small patties. Heat oil in fry pan. Fry both sides until golden brown. Take out of oil and place on paper towel. To serve, top your fry bread with chili, cooked ground beef, cheese, tomatoes, lettuce, and any other taco fixings of your choice.

UKRAINE
VARENIKI
• 1 3/4 Cup flour
• 2 eggs
• 3/4 teaspoon salt
• 1/4 Cup water

Add ingredients together and knead dough. Cover and let sit 1 hour. Meanwhile prepare filling. Fillings could be mashed potatoes, crumbled or shredded meat, cooked, sautéed mushrooms, sauerkraut, or the cheese filling below.
• 8 oz. cottage cheese
• 1 egg
• Pinch of salt and pepper

To assemble Vareniki roll out dough to ¼ inch thin. Cut out with a round biscuit cutter or the top of a glass. Put 1 Tablespoon filling on each circle. Wet the edges with a finger dipped in water. Press edges together. Cook in boiling water until they float to the top about 5 minutes. Fry in butter or oil or serve as is drizzled with olive oil

HOLLAND
OLIE-KOECKEN (DUTCH DONUTS)
- 3 packages dry yeast
- 1/2 Cup warm water
- 8 Tablespoons melted butter
- 1 3/4 Cups raisins
- 4 Cups flour
- 1/4 teaspoon salt
- 1 Tablespoon cinnamon
- 1/2 teaspoon cloves
- 1/2 teaspoon ground ginger
- 1 1/2 Cups milk
- 3 apples peeled and shredded
- 1 Cup whole almonds
- Oil for deep-frying

Add yeast to your warm water and add a pinch of sugar. Let sit several minutes. Add to mixing bowl. Place raisins in a bowl and pour boiling water over the top and let sit several minutes. Meanwhile add flour, salt, cinnamon, cloves, and ginger to a mixing bowl. Add melted butter, yeast, and milk. Stir to combine. Add raisins, shredded apples, and almonds. Knead together and cover your bowl with a towel. Let rise for 1 hour. After 1 hour, heat oil in a pan until 350 degrees. Add a tablespoon of dough into your heated oil, being careful not to splatter your hot oil. Fry each side until golden brown. Place on paper towels to drain. Add 1 Cup of powdered sugar to a small bowl. Roll doughnuts in powdered sugar.

THAILAND

THAI CURRIED RICE

- Oil
- 1 garlic clove, minced
- 1 onion, chopped
- 2 Cups cooked white rice
- 1 potato diced and boiled
- ¼ Cup peas
- 3 Tablespoons soy sauce
- ½ teaspoon brown or white sugar
- 1 teaspoon curry powder

In oil, sauté garlic and onion. Stir in cooked rice, cooked potatoes, peas, soy sauce, sugar, and curry powder. Stir to combine. Heat several minutes and serve.

PHILIPPINES
SIMPLE LUMPIAS
• Lumpia wrappers
• Cooked ground beef
• 2-3 carrots, shredded

Mix cooked beef and carrots together in bowl. Season with salt and pepper. Heat a small pan of oil on the stove to deep fat fry. Or you can bake this in the oven. Place 1-2 tablespoons of beef mixture on end of a lumpia wrapper. Roll up and tuck in sides. Continue to roll to the end. Seal the seam with a finger that has been dipped in water. Fry in oil until crispy.
Serve with teriyaki sauce or other dipping sauce.

**Another simple filling idea is cooked shredded chicken seasoned with 1-2 tablespoons soy sauce
and a sprinkle of ginger. (Or to taste.)

AFRICA

SQUASH AND YAMS

- 1 onion, chopped
- Oil
- 1 squash peeled and cut into cubes
- 2 yams, peeled and cut into cubes
- 1 Cup coconut milk
- 1/2 teaspoon cinnamon
- 1/4 teaspoon ground cloves

In large saucepan or pot sauté onion in oil. Add squash, yams, and milk. Bring to a boil. Turn to medium low and cover with a lid. Allow to simmer 5-10 minutes or until squash and yams are tender. Add cinnamon, cloves, salt, and pepper before serving.

WESTERN USA
TEXAS TOAST
- Chili, prepared
- Shredded cheese
- Thick slices of bread

Layer bread slices on a cookie sheet and bake at 450 degrees for 5-10 minutes until well toasted. Or if you are only doing a few slices use the toaster. Spread warm chili on top of toast and sprinkle with cheese. If your chili is hot, it will help melt the cheese.

Made in the USA
Las Vegas, NV
21 July 2023

75065132R00103